D1431582

Left-Handed Liberty

In his latest play John Arden breathes new life into the old story of a villainous king brought to bay by villainous barons. His theme is liberty: and what interests him more than the events leading up to Runnymede is the failure of the Charter after it was signed. The agreement on paper could not be valid until it had taken place in the minds of both King John and the barons.

Left-Handed Liberty

A PLAY ABOUT MAGNA CARTA

BY

JOHN ARDEN

LONDON
METHUEN & CO LTD
11 NEW FETTER LANE EC4

This play is fully protected by copyright.
All inquiries concerning performing rights
should be directed to Theatrework (London) Ltd,
22 Hans Road, London SW3

First published 1965
© 1965 *by John Arden*
All rights reserved
Printed in Great Britain by
the Shenval Press
London, Hertford and Harlow

Notes on the Characters

JOHN   Aged forty-eight in 1215, but seems older. Corpulent, short, with dark hair turning to grey and going bald, well-trimmed beard, a grinning wolfish mouth full of bad teeth. Very energetic but out of condition. His moods fluctuate unnervingly. Terrifying in his anger, but can also be jovial and generous – not always in order to deceive.

ISABELLE   The ladies in this play are dimly-glimpsed, but the subject makes this difficult to avoid. The Queen is in her late twenties, of a delicate beauty, a warm and dreamy personality.

ELEANOR   Eighty-two years old, which is very old indeed by the standards of the time. Has been a fascinating dark Mediterranean beauty who has introduced into Western thought and poetry the concept of chivalry in the service of romantic love.

HENRY   He does not have to speak: but is a doll-like royal child who takes more after his mother than his father.

ARCHBISHOP   In late middle age – intellectual, strong-minded, passionate in pursuit of what he conceives to be right. What would now be called a 'progressive' churchman, in contrast to –

PANDULPH   who is dogmatic, sly, politically tough, but despising politics. An elderly man whose spiritual life is as deep as his worldly involvements are dubious. Not a man to make fun of, whatever one may think of his ideas.

MARSHAL   Over seventy – a great age for an active soldier and statesman. Handsome, unimaginative, a paragon of the

v

conservative virtues.

YOUNG MARSHAL   In his twenties. Much like his father – chivalrous and earnest though not so easily shocked.

FITZWALTER   A bull-necked fighter in the prime of life, unscrupulous and insensitively cynical.

DE VESCI   Like Fitzwalter, but with a neurotic edge to him, particularly where his personal concerns are in question, and rather more intelligent.

LADY DE VESCI   Late twenties, a strong young woman with a sense of satire and not easily humiliated. A reserved disposition.

THE MAYOR OF LONDON   A serious-minded businessman, who is a little cowed by the responsibilities he has taken on and the company he finds himself in: but determined none the less to stand up for himself and his city.

THE CLERK   Although in Holy Orders he has the job of a civil servant and his professional mannerisms do not differ greatly from those to be found in Whitehall today. Aged about thirty.

PHILIP   Seen only as a political persona – a walking statue of Kingship, with no personal idiosyncrasies to blur the picture.

LOUIS   As his father: but in a state of aspiration rather than fulfilment.

BLANCHE   A cold fat greedy slug of a lady, and unfortunately the exigencies of the plot prevent any further understanding of her.

THE GIRLS   Strident in dress, coarse in voice. The blonde one is fat – otherwise they are mainly distinguished one from the other by the colours of their hair, which should be clearly artificial – wigs or violent dyes. All three are very young. The DARK and RED-HAIRED GIRLS, who have to appear in Act III as street entertainers, should dress for this part of their rôles in a gipsified fashion – all ribbons and trinkets.

GOLDSMITH   A thin mean bilious man, late forties, dressed in good clothes which have been worn threadbare.

GOLDSMITH'S WIFE   Early twenties, foolish, amorous; domesticated and demure despite her equivocal way of life.

PARSON   A well-built rubicund, Friar-Tuck sort of fellow – the fool of the family put into the Church.

BARONS in general   These have nothing much to say but should give the impression of resolute soldierly competence unspoilt by much refinement.

OFFICERS AND SOLDIERS   These are John's brutal Flemings – battle-scarred professionals of immense aptitude at their trade.

Author's Notes

There is very little in this play which cannot be justified historically. I have had to sandwich events here and there and transpose a few episodes, but I have only invented – as far as I can be sure – Pandulph's correspondence on behalf of the King with the Flemish recruiting agent; Young Marshal's love for Lady de Vesci; the episode at Dover with the Goldsmith and his Wife; and Lady de Vesci's relationship with John. The latter intrigue is supposed to have taken place at an earlier date in John's reign, and in fact to have been foiled by the substitution of a woman of the lower orders, in the manner of a folk-tale. But John was often accused of seducing the wives of his nobility – he is also said to have violated Fitzwalter's daughter – and the story is convenient for the play, so I put it in. Pandulph's correspondence certainly took place at the hands of somebody, and the role of the Papal Legate was sufficiently invidious at this time for my version to be plausible. Young Marshal may or may not have fallen in love with another Baron's wife – such behaviour was regarded as a necessary part of a young knight's emotional development. The King's Justice at Dover is a fictional but not untypical example of John's high-handed and humorous way of handling such situations. The tension I have suggested between the Barons and the City of London is not actually described in history, though Roger of Wendover (a baronial partisan) does accuse the leaders of the 'Army of God' of 'playing at damnable dice, selecting for themselves the best wine for drinking, and practising who knows what besides'. If this was so, it is probable that their relations with the City Fathers would not have been of the best.

The above notes refer to the *facts* contained in the play. The *opinions* are perhaps less historical. It is difficult to know exactly what thirteenth century statesmen and clerics were thinking about most of the time – the chronicles of the period are usually bald and prejudiced. John himself was very roughly handled by their compilers, largely because he had quarrelled with the Church in the earlier part of his reign: and even though, by the time of the Charter, the Pope and he were reconciled, the English clergy continued to vilify him. It seems unlikely, however, that any of the men concerned with drawing up the Great Charter had any conception of the reputation the document would have for future generations. They no doubt believed that they were defining an uncertain and disputed frontier between the rights of the king and those of his subjects; and any idea that they were preparing 'the cornerstone of English liberty' must have been far from their minds. Indeed it was far from the minds of any Englishmen until about the end of the sixteenth century. The great lawyer Coke, in the reign of James I, used the Charter as an authority for his attacks upon the royal prerogative: and during the disputes between Charles I and Parliament it was frequently referred to and acclaimed as a general statement of libertarian principle – not always very honestly – but any stick is good enough to beat a tyrant with, it might well have been thought. Since then, this view of the Charter has obtained, though modern historians have done their best to correct it. But most people remember little of mediaeval history from their schooldays, and the picturesque image of the villainous king, brought to bay upon the banks of the Thames one sunny day in June, sticks in the minds of many who in their own lives would not dream of adopting so unsophisticated an attitude towards political reform.

Nevertheless, the 'cornerstone' theory has something to be said for it. If Coke and the seventeenth century parliamentarians were able to 'misuse' the Charter so effectively, they gave to it an importance which is not diminished by being shewn to be unthought-of in the days of John. Of course, much of the document is now entirely out of date. Clauses relating to the minutiae of feudal service and such purely local grievances as fish-weirs in the Thames have dropped out of the national memory. The general principles of 'no imprisonment without judgement by one's peers' and 'no denial or sale of justice' may not have meant in 1215 quite what we take them to mean today – indeed, they were not *principles* at all in 1215: but have since been elevated to that status. This is due, no doubt, to the very convenient generality of the language in which they are expressed. I have in the play allowed King John to claim this as his own inspiration – there is no evidence that it was: but on the other hand no evidence that it was not. The form of the Charter was decided upon after considerable negotiation with the king: and no doubt he did succeed in getting the wording changed here and there. Perhaps I view his character and motives too favourably. It is difficult, however, to resist the rather weird charm of any of the Plantagenets when one comes to examine their personalities at close range. Even the worst of them – and it is hard to find any other category for John, with the best will in the world – seem to have stood head and shoulders above most of their contemporaries, at least in the political field.

When I accepted this commission, I knew little more about the Charter than what I had been taught at the age of fourteen. It was a considerable surprise for me to discover how soon the agreement between John and the Barons was repudiated, and how unfortunate his reconciliation with the Pope had proved for the Baronial party. This apparent complete failure of the Charter struck me as a more fruitful theme for a play than the more obvious one of the events leading up to Runnymede. If this play has any direct message – and I am not normally an enthusiast for didactic drama – I suppose it is that an agreement on paper is worth nothing to anybody unless it has taken place in their minds as well: and that if we want liberty we have to make quite sure that

(a) We know what sort of liberty we are fighting for:
(b) Our methods of fighting are not such as to render that liberty invalid before we even attain it:
(c) We understand that we are in more danger of losing it once we have attained it than if we had never had it; which is an Irishism, but clear enough for all that.

A final point: the City of London. This play has been commissioned by the descendants of the City Fathers of King John's day. I hope that they will not be disappointed by the not very glorious rôle played by the Lord Mayor of that time. I cannot however do anything about this. He was associated with the Barons in a subordinate capacity and as this was the first time that the commercial middle class took an active part in English politics it is to be expected that its attitude would have been fairly tentative. The unattractive portrayal of the Baronial leaders is fully justified by history: fortunately idealism was present on their side in the person of Archbishop Langton. I have tried to make the Mayor more akin to the Archbishop than to Fitzwalter: which is the best I can do for him, as he is not known to have initiated any active deeds or policy.

The Language of the Play. Most of the characters would have conversed in Norman French or (in the case of Pandulph, for example, who was an Italian) in Latin. The lower and middle class people would have spoken old English. I have no idea what tongue would be employed in a conversation, say, between Lord de Vesci and a prostitute in London. Probably Londoners were nearly all able to manage a little French, and most nobles who lived away from the Court could at least

summon up a few words of English for agricultural, military
or sexual purposes.

Therefore I have tried to write a kind of dialogue which has
the straightforwardness of mediaeval speech – more florid
for courtly scenes and more colloquial for other episodes, but
generally without regional colouring. De Vesci was a North-
umbrian lord, and quite possibly spoke his French with an
accent different from that of the King, whose contacts were as
much with France as England – but it is no doubt safer to
ignore this. Similarly the Mayor of London and the three Girls
should not be allowed to be too cockney, nor should the people
of Dover become involved with a Kentish burr. Certainly
Pandulph must not be a stage-Italian, and Lady de Vesci –
although Scots by birth – belongs like her husband to the
prevailing Norman culture.

Details of Staging. I do not think much scenery is involved or
should be involved. The main requirements are a chair for
Pandulph at the front of the stage, right in one corner (where
he can sit throughout certain scenes without being too
obvious: and yet the audience must be aware that he is there)
and a frame or easel in the corresponding position on the
opposite side of the stage where the emblems for each act
(chart, parchment, and map of England) are hung. These
emblems should be as large as is convenient, and drawn or
written, in a plausible mediaeval style. The chair is similar to
a bishop's throne in a cathedral, with a Gothic canopy and a
reading desk. The desk can serve to conceal the various props
that Pandulph needs while he is there, and when he has
nothing else to do – particularly during John's long speech in
Act III – he should be busy with books and papers upon it.

In the centre of the main stage is an area curtained-off,
which is to be used for the discovery of persons and furniture
where necessary. This area should project forward into the

acting area, and be surrounded on three sides by drapes which might well be of a rich tapestry-material, appropriate to the period. There is no need for these drapes to be taller than, say, eight or nine feet. Above them, and in the same plane, is suspended a screen for the projection of the scene-emblems – the views of Runnymede, London river etc. These pictures I imagine drawn in the style of thirteenth century MS illuminations. Certainly they must not be realistic. If real pictures of the period are available, so much the better.

Otherwise the stage is to be bare, and the furniture should be kept to an absolute minimum.

J.A.

Left-Handed Liberty was commissioned by the Corporation of the City of London to commemorate the 750th Anniversary of the sealing of Magna Carta.

The first public performance was given on Monday, 14th June, 1965, at the Mermaid Theatre, Puddle Dock, London, following its presentation to invited audiences under the auspices of the Corporation during the week 7th to 12th June, 1965. The cast was as follows:

KING JOHN	Patrick Wymark
ISABELLE his Wife	Jennifer Clulow
ELEANOR OF AQUITAINE his Mother	Sonia Dresdel
PRINCE HENRY his Son	Roy Hills
STEPHEN LANGTON, Archbishop of Canterbury	
	Bernard Miles
PANDULPH the Papal Legate	Robert Eddison
WILLIAM MARSHAL, Earl of Pembroke	Esmond Knight
YOUNG MARSHAL his Son	Eric Allan
ROBERT FITZWALTER ⎫ Leaders of the	Freddie Jones
EUSTACE DE VESCI ⎬ Baronial Party	Timothy Bateson
LADY DE VESCI	Barbara Mitchell
MAYOR OF LONDON	Redmond Phillips
PHILIP, King of France	Colin Ellis
LOUIS his Son	Jeremy Rowe
BLANCHE, Wife of Louis	Liane Aukin
THREE WHORES	Sally Miles
	Denise Coffey
	Janet Gahan
A GOLDSMITH	Frederick Hall
His WIFE	Denise Coffey
A PARSON	Ronald Herdman
A CLERK of the Royal Household	Colin Ellis

Barons, Clerks, Servants, Ladies in Waiting, Officers, etc.

Terry Adams	Ronald Cunliffe	Ronald Herdman
Edward Argent	Robert Gillespie	Douglas Milvain
Roger Bizley	Michael Gleave	Adrian Reynolds
John Bloomfield	Christina Greatrex	Georgina Simpson

Directed by David William
Designed by Adrian Vaux
Costumes designed by Robin Pidcock

Act One

A chart opposite PANDULPH's *chair shewing the world and the heavenly bodies. House lights still up.*

Enter PANDULPH.

PANDULPH. Let me explain very briefly that progress in the affairs of this world has ceased to exist. That is to say, there has been progress: there have been certain cardinal events. Eve in Eden ate her fruit and then she fell and her man fell, and they discovered how naked they were. Later the Deluge, God promised it would not occur again and it did not, and after that . . . well, you may read your Bibles, it is all there. So, after many degenerate and bewildered generations, the Master of the Vineyard sent His Son to inspect the work. The disaffected workmen nailed Him up, upon the trellis of their own neglected vines, and were astonished when He was not dead. God, who had moved throughout human history, moved out at last for ever – no, not for ever. He will come once more, one day, when? I do not know. Maybe tomorrow morning, before you even reach your places of work; but in the meantime He is not here. He has left His representative, the Church. The Church is central to human life, as the world itself is central to the organization of the universe –

He refers to the chart:

There is the world; the moon, and the planets, revolve in their spheres – there is the exterior sphere upon the inner surface of which the myriad stars are painted or embossed or perhaps are but little openings pricked out by God's finger to let in the light of Heaven. And here is Heaven. Hell: Purgatory: Limbo. Very good.

B

Now, as the world is the centre of the whole created system, so Jerusalem, God's Holy City, is the centre of the world – but Jerusalem, as you know, is held by the infidel. The late King Richard Lionheart endeavoured to relieve it, but failed. Therefore the temporary or acting centre of the world may be taken to be Rome, which is appropriate because of the prior example of the Caesars – and the nations of Christendom revolve around the Roman citadel of Christ's own Vicar, just as these outer planets, here, revolve around the world.

As we can expect in our affairs no further direct intervention of Divinity until the Second Coming, and as, without Divinity, man is little more than meat bones and water on the slab of a butcher's shop, it must therefore be clear that no alternation, no betterment, no human improvement, no progress is going to be possible: unless it comes through the Church or the Saints of the Church. Which would be intervention indeed, but indirect and inevitably spiritual rather than material. If the Church were to concern Herself with material circumstances She would be usurping the prerogative of God's own directness, fabricating illegitimately a second Deluge perhaps, or rewriting the Ten Commandments, already divinely and immutably engraved, or occupying Herself with a new tidal wave in an unauthorized Red Sea.

So therefore we concern ourselves only with the sins and repentance of individual men, and, instructed by Our Lord, take no thought for the morrow, what raiment we should put on or what food we should consume, or how we should organize the government of nations. John, King of England, Lord of Ireland, Duke of Normandy, born Anno Domini 1167, is an anointed King and therefore requires the obedience of his subjects. That is all the Church has to say upon the matter. His widowed mother, of course, being of a subordinate yet blessed sex, may choose to say more, but

remember the words of Jesus: 'Woman, what have I to do with thee? My hour is not yet come'.
A Castle in Aquitaine, 1204.

He resumes his seat.

Act One

SCENE ONE

A figure of the Virgin and Child.

ELEANOR *discovered on a throne, wrapped in furs.* JOHN *enters and makes obeisance.*

ELEANOR. Our son was late. Very late. Two hours late.

JOHN. I have already apologized, mother, with (I thought) a very fair address of courtesy. Matters of state, matters of alarm of state, detained me, and the roads were extremely bad. (*He calls to someone offstage.*) Tell my Clerk of Works it is time they were attended to! But I have arrived in your hall, I was not too late for the consumption of wine and spices.

ELEANOR. No. And with a very fair address of courtesy. Queens are susceptible to it. Stone walls have never heard of it. For our son has been late elsewhere, has he not? He failed to save his castle from the enemy. Saucy Castle on the borders of Normandy. The King of France flies banners from the roof. We in Aquitaine have heard that news already. Normandy tomorrow will belong to France. Our son, who was the Duke of it, our son who is the King, was late. Landless John, his father called him, because he gave him no portion when he was born. Now that he has inherited to the full the portions of all those other sons who came into the world before him, and who left it before him in their time and in the time of God, he should be no longer landless. Yet we have heard there are some who still describe him so. They name him Bluntsword also, King Softblade, is it not?

JOHN. Or even King Slapstick – that is one way I have heard it put. Very funny. Malicious. But I would not call it true. The military circumstances are –

ELEANOR. Our husband King Henry could have been the greatest king that the English ever had. King William the Bastard, for all his cruelty, was not a greater than he. Because William was but self-sufficient, by himself alone he conquered himself his kingdom: he ruled it by himself for fifteen years until the King of France one day laughed at his huge belly and called him a pregnant woman. William, being by himself, had nobody to laugh with when France chose to laugh *at* him, and in his impotent and childish anger he burst his poor huge belly and that was the end of him. Sufficient in the end for nothing but a mortal loss of temper. He should have had a wife.

JOHN. His children were legitimate – he did have a wife.

ELEANOR. He should have had a wife to laugh with him and to laugh at him instead of that unfortunate lady who spoke two words to him once, and having incontinently been dragged by the hair of her head at the tail of his horse from one end of the city to the other, preferred ever after to remain silent.

JOHN. He did have a wife. *I* have a wife.

ELEANOR. Did you speak?

JOHN. I said I have a wife, mother.

ELEANOR. Your father had a wife. He was about to have been the greatest king the English had ever heard of, but he decided to be self-sufficient, and he dispensed with his wife. Why, he put her into prison. He divided by force the twin flesh that had been made one, and the sons of her poor huge belly turned upon him with their adolescent chaos, and it burst his own belly for him and that was the end of him. John.

JOHN. Yes, mother: I am attentive, mother.

ELEANOR. John. I am very old. And I am sitting so unnaturally still and so upright because if I were to move I think I should fall down. I am waiting for someone to come and take me away. When he comes he must find me elegant, in the manner of my youth.

He will break down the door –

JOHN (*calling to someone offstage*). The Queen is ill, she
    requires attendance –

ELEANOR.

He will break down the door.

He must not find me lying on the floor.

He is the only one

Who is sufficient. He is alone.

You are alone, my landless bluntsword son.

The disciple whom Jesus loved, they called him John.

Into his care walked the Lady Mary slowly

Slow, easy, secret, so arrogant she seemed so lowly,

She went around where he breaks in.

He will break in and I will go with him.

Slowly and gently and he will be ashamed of his breaking.

What way will you go?

After what manner are you making?

JOHN.

I am making what I want to make

In the manner I want to make it.

The English are mine

And what I want I shall take it,

Or provide it, when I want,

In the manner of my father.

ELEANOR.

The manner of your mother

Is always much better.

Hide behind the corner

Dictate a polite letter.

So if it has to be done, do it easily and quietly,

Afterwards deny it.

No-one need know it.

Sometimes for my lover

Sometimes for my poet

Always I kept the back door unlocked

Never for the King:
He could beat at the great gate
Until the hinges rocked.
John. John. On your left hand
Wear your most beautiful ring
And do not let it show.
The military circumstances
Enforce you to be slow
But you must never be late.

Where is my visitor? I was expecting him . . . It is dis-
courteous to be so unpunctual when an old lady is waiting . . .

    ELEANOR *is hidden from view.*
    Next scene to follow immediately.

SCENE TWO

The Papal Arms.
    JOHN *comes downstage.*

JOHN. My mother, Queen Eleanor of Aquitaine, received her
tardy visitor upon April the first, 1204 – they call it All
Fools' Day in England. And we buried her at Fontrevault. She
was eighty-two years old. However rudely death came in unto
her, and however directly he attempted to force her to walk,
I have no doubt but that she remembered the name of the
day and made a fool of him in the passage. Not on the first
of April, but on the nineteenth of June, some eleven years
later, there came together a large number of my subjects to
try to make a fool of me – being, as I was, the son of
a meandering mother, and for that matter, the son of my
father, who would never be governed, never –

PANDULPH. Your Grace, you have omitted something.

JOHN. Am I corrected? Does someone dare? Ah, Master
Pandulph: The Legate of the Pope. (*He looks at* PAN-
DULPH'S *chart.*) I mistrust these geometrical figures,
Pandulph. They are altogether too pat. If one of these

circles here were to have a little kink in it, thus – you would find perhaps Mars banging into Venus at a vulnerable and tender point and your entirely perfect mechanism would be wrecked by eccentricity.

PANDULPH. Exactly so. *If* there were a kink. But a kink would be a falsehood, and a falsehood in the geometry of God is inconceivable. But you are not the geometry of God, Your Grace, you are a mortal man and very prone to falsehood. As I said, you have omitted something. In your account of your stewardship of the remote English vineyard, you failed to mention, did you not, that for six whole years you yourself were excommunicate and your kingdom laid under Interdict. You chose to defy the Pope –

JOHN. Over a technical matter –

PANDULPH. The appointment of an Archbishop. Technical? Perhaps. But in the end, you were governed. You were compelled to submit.

JOHN. I chose to submit. I viewed the matter in a larger perspective. I never make the mistake of elevating small disputes into questions of principle. Besides, I had to deal with Baronial discontent and a danger of invasion from France.

PANDULPH. Nevertheless, you surrendered your crown to the Pope and received it back, upon terms. Here it is. (*He holds up the crown.*)

JOHN. I am glad to get it back. All my jewels are beautiful, this more beautiful than most, quite apart from its significance. You haven't abstracted any of the decorations, have you? No: that is just as well.

PANDULPH (*withdrawing crown from* JOHN's *reach*). Kneel, my son, and acknowledge your fault.

JOHN. Under pressure, and with all due calculation, I will kneel. (*He does so.*)

Having offended God and our Mother the Holy Church in many things, and hence being in great need of the Divine

Mercy, we offer and freely yield to God and to the Lord Pope Innocent III and his catholic successors, the whole kingdom of England for the remission of our sins, so that from henceforth we hold it from him and from the Holy Roman Church our Mother, as a sworn vassal. And let this Charter of Obligation remain for ever valid.

PANDULPH. Come then, exalted Prince, fulfil the promises given and confirm the concessions offered, so that God Almighty may ever fulfil any righteous desire of yours, enabling you so to walk amid temporal blessings as not to fail of winning the eternal.

He places the crown on JOHN's *head.*

JOHN (*standing up*). And furthermore I swear that as soon as I have the means and opportunity I will lead an army to the Holy Land and redeem from the Paynim Turk, by force, the Blessed Sepulchre of Christ.

PANDULPH (*producing a jewelled cross*). Wear this upon your breast in token of your sanctified intention. (*He hangs the cross round* JOHN's *neck.*)

JOHN. Diamonds? Good. Silver-gilt. Not so good. Parsimonious, rather.

PANDULPH. Make sure you keep your word. The Pope is a man of honour, he expects his vassals to be likewise.

JOHN. He has evidently little experience of the sort of vassal that I am lumbered with.

1215: a meadow upon the bank of the Thames, between Staines and Windsor: Runnymede.

SCENE THREE

A picture of pavilions, flags, men-at-arms, with a field full of flowers and the river curling round.

CLERKS *arranging a table and a throne, and preparing the apparatus for moulding the royal seal. Copies of the Charter.*

Enter MARSHAL.

JOHN (*to* CLERK). Put that table facing north: I want the light behind me.

MARSHAL. Sire.

JOHN. Marshal.

MARSHAL. It is the nineteenth of June.

JOHN. I do believe it is.

MARSHAL. Your loyal barons, sire, desire to know –

JOHN. My *what*, sir?

MARSHAL. I was endeavouring to apply a correct and decorous courtesy to a situation that is already –

JOHN. But they are not loyal, are they, Marshal?

MARSHAL. No.

JOHN. Then God's Feet, do not call them so! They are in armed rebellion against me, sir, they have captured my castles, they have refused to pay me my taxes, they have colleagued themselves, Marshal, in a treasonable conspiracy and withdrawn their oaths of fealty. A correct courtesy to such runagates is to cut off their testicles. I am very well aware that you are regarded as the ancient arbiter of chivalry in this kingdom, but to be so scrupulous in your terms is to speak with two tongues in one mouth, which is dishonest and I will not have it. Honesty, William, above everything, when conferring with your King. My barons, you were about to say, desire to know – what?

MARSHAL. Whether you intend to confirm the Charter of Liberties you were so gracious as to approve, provisionally, four days ago. I would remind you, sire, that the barons agreed a truce with you until the beginning of this week, and for no longer. It is now Friday.

JOHN. They have more soldiers than I have. They insisted as a condition of truce that I disband my Flemish mercenaries. I suggested in return that as an earnest of good faith they should disband their own levies.

MARSHAL. They have not done so.

JOHN. No. But on the other hand, William, their army has

been raised from the peasants on their estates. It is very
nearly harvest time. They will have to let them go home or
they will have no food all winter. My men can come back
from Flanders any time I care to whistle. Mine is a good
policy to employ professionals where possible. They fight
better, too.

MARSHAL. This is beside the point, is it not? The barons
require an answer.

JOHN. Oh yes. So they do. We are not yet entirely satisfied,
Marshal, with the terms of this document. The final clause
in it provides for a committee of – let me refresh my
memory – (*he picks up a copy of the Charter*) yes, twenty-
five barons,

'Who must, with all their might observe, hold, and cause to
be observed, the peace and liberties which we have granted
by this present Charter.'

And so forth. Now – quis custodiet ipsos custodes? And,
even more pertinently, who are to be the ipsos custodes?

MARSHAL. The Archbishop has suggested that a further
thirty-eight barons should assist and partly control the
twenty-five delegated. As to the composition of the twenty-
five themselves, I am afraid –

JOHN. I too am afraid, sir. They will select the most traitorous
and self-aggrandizing cormorants out of all their rebellious
crew! Eustace de Vesci, Robert Fitzwalter, are they in the
list?

MARSHAL. They are, but –

JOHN. And you have a son of your own, Marshal, what about
him?

MARSHAL. Sire, my most unworthy headstrong son –

JOHN. Is leagued against his King. He has fallen into bad
company, has he not, Marshal? Twenty-five over-kings to
control the King of England. Do they desire me to cut my
crown into two dozen and more pieces and distribute it
among them?

MARSHAL. It was intended as no more than a safeguard, sire.

JOHN. A safeguard against what?

MARSHAL. Bad faith.

> *Enter* ARCHBISHOP. *He bows curtly to* JOHN, *who ignores him.*

JOHN. Whose bad faith? Oh William, I am an old man, grey-headed, fat . . .

MARSHAL. Sire –

JOHN. Not so old as you, of course. That would be difficult. After all, you were, as it were, my father's tutor, if not my grandfather's . . . But none the less, I am old. My memory is failing. So explain to me, my dear and faithful friend – how in the Name of God did all this turbulence begin?

MARSHAL. I suppose it began with the fall of Saucy Castle.

JOHN. And the loss of my French possessions. In order to retain them, I had to make wars. In order to make wars, I needed an army. The provision of such an army is the business of my barons, in return for which they hold their lands. But, as we have discovered, their men must go home to gather in the harvest, so instead I hire mercenaries, and mercenaries must be paid. So I demand from the barons a regular contribution known as the shield-tax, which has been accepted for generations as an adequate substitute for the sending of troops. And by God they refuse it me!

MARSHAL. Your shield-taxes were excessive, sire.

ARCHBISHOP. Not even your brother King Richard, with all the expenses of the Crusade –

JOHN. I am not my brother. (Archbishop, good morning, we are glad to see you here.) Nor is this year last year. And the price of goods and services increases unaccountably. We need a kink in the circle, do we not, Pandulph? Or possibly your immutable geometry does not take into consideration the ups and downs of money. Which are caused by the corn-harvest in Brittany or the wool-trade in Germany or something to do with the Jews – I don't know: do you know?

William here has never even thought about it, have you,
William? But my soldiers demand to be paid.

MARSHAL. Your soldiers lost their battles, sire. The battles
were in France. The barons of England see but small reason –

JOHN. Why they should be asked to protect the territories of
their king. It all amounts to that. A grotesque lack of
loyalty. And even defeated soldiers still demand to be paid.
I keep to my bargains. Which is more than Richard did. For
who holds Jerusalem? He swore that he would liberate it.
The infidel is still there. But not for long. Our purpose is
declared. It is generally accepted, I think, as being a worthy
purpose.

ARCHBISHOP. If the Crusader himself is worthy, his worth is
increased by that of his purpose. If he is not worthy –

PANDULPH. Insofar as he is a Crusader, he is to be deemed
worthy, my Lord. It is akin to the vocation of a priest. A
sacrament administered by a fornicator, for example, is
nevertheless a valid endowment of Grace. The point is
elementary, but –

ARCHBISHOP. We need not dispute it here. This morning it is
not relevant.

JOHN. Oh yes it is.

ARCHBISHOP. Sire, it is not relevant. The barons expect an
immediate answer. Are you or are you not prepared to
confirm their Charter?

JOHN. As far as it goes, Archbishop, it is a very good Charter.

ARCHBISHOP. I hope so. I drew most of it up myself. I
managed to restrain the more unjust of their demands.

JOHN. Indeed you did, and you are very loyal. Some of it is
excellent. Listen to this:
   'To no-one will we sell, to no-one will we refuse or delay
   right and justice.'
This clause cuts both ways. *I* have always respected the
Laws and the Customs of England, and I have never
refused justice. Sometimes the barons have. Now they will

not be able to, nor will anyone else. Good. And this, as well: 'No free man shall be arrested or imprisoned or deprived of his freehold or outlawed or exiled or in any way destroyed, neither will we set forth against him or send against him, except by the lawful judgement of his peers and the law of the land.'
Have I ever attempted to do any of that?

MARSHAL. Sometimes, sire, it has – seemed so.

JOHN. The king in his own kingdom is surely permitted to seem. Whether what he seems and what he is, are identical, is quite another matter. If the barons as well as the King shall pay heed to that clause, this land will be a Paradise for those that inhabit it. What about this one?
'The City of London shall have all its ancient liberties and free customs as well by land as by water.'
I have always been most careful to cherish the City of London – when they built their new bridge across the river I provided them the architect. How can they walk now from Thames Street into Southwark without thinking of their King in shame? And no longer time ago than the beginning of last month, why, I granted them a Charter!

ARCHBISHOP. You tried to buy them with a Charter.

JOHN. What! Very well, it was a bribe. I needed their loyalty. Yet such is the gratitude of the commercial classes, that almost immediately they threw open their gates to the Baronial Forces. And yet it was, was it not, an idiotic treachery? The interests of trade and the interests of nobility have always been disparate.

ARCHBISHOP. Good government under secure law is in the interests of all classes, my lord.

JOHN. In the interests of all classes with power in their hands, yes . . . Never mind, never mind it now. I suppose the Mayor of London may retain his ancient liberties – provided that he tells this garrison to get out. Is he going to tell them?

ARCHBISHOP. I will tell them, sire. There will be two sides to this agreement.

JOHN. There had better be, I think.

MARSHAL. We must trust to the honour of the barons. They are men of Christian chivalry and I cannot believe –

JOHN. I can. Twenty-five of them, on the evidence of their past history neither Christian nor chivalrous, are to supervise the enforcement of this Charter. We do not like their names and we do not like their intentions. We are not at all sure that we will grant them permission to supervise anything at all. Trust to their honour indeed. I judge men's honour by the standards of my own: and I know how much of the commodity I am able to afford. Will you never learn that a straightforward king is a dead king? You understand about it, don't you, Master Legate – you've seen the orbs and sceptres topple in your time.

PANDULPH. All flesh is grass, certainly.

ARCHBISHOP. But the Laws of God are immutable and the virtuous man –

JOHN. Is nonetheless a free being. And which of us dare predict how or in what direction we are going to sin next? I have a little mistress and last night she deceived me with a cook-boy from my kitchen. If I were the tyrannical Tiberius my loyal barons would have you believe, I would have put out her eyes. Instead, I went to bed with my wife. They are coming here at noon, are they not? I may condescend to receive them, I may even agree with them. On the other hand, perhaps I won't. The King, in fact, will Advise Himself. You must be patient and wait for him . . . (*He is going out, but stops and addresses a* CLERK.) What's your name?

CLERK. Augustine, my Lord.

JOHN. Then you are named after a strange fellow. St Augustine of Hippo. Altogether too penitent. He enjoyed his sins while he committed them: he should have been grateful later for the pleasure he had obtained. It is never too late to give thanks.

Exit JOHN.

MARSHAL. What do you think he intends to do?

ARCHBISHOP. William, he has told you. He intends to advise himself.

MARSHAL. You really believe he has not yet made up his mind?

ARCHBISHOP. I do not believe he has ever made up his mind.

MARSHAL. But surely he cannot repudiate his promises at this stage of the business? He has already sealed a provisional draft of the barons' demands. His honour is committed, Archbishop.

ARCHBISHOP. Yes.

PANDULPH. (*to* CLERK). What are you doing?

CLERK. Making copies of the Charter, sir: and preparing the wax for the seal.

PANDULPH. Upon whose instructions?

CLERK. Upon the King's instructions, sir.

MARSHAL. Surely he would not have ordered these preparations, had he not intended to –

ARCHBISHOP. He has also ordered preparations for undertaking a Crusade.

MARSHAL. Not very serious ones.

ARCHBISHOP. The work of two or three clerks at copying out documents is not necessarily very serious either.

PANDULPH. And yet if he does intend to confirm the Charter, this work will be needed. We should not ignore it. Nor should we ignore the possibility of a Crusade, my Lord Archbishop. The Pope does not ignore it.

ARCHBISHOP. I regret to say the Pope has very little understanding of what goes on in this country, Master Pandulph.

PANDULPH. The Pope had sufficient understanding to appoint you Archbishop, your Grace, at a time when the King had another man in mind and the monks of Canterbury yet another. I did not think that *you* would question the wisdom of His Holiness.

ARCHBISHOP. The wisdom of His Holiness cost England six
    years of Interdiction. The King, who is a proud man, had
    to face a humiliating reversal of all that he had striven for,
    and I myself, despite my Archbishopric, have suffered
    untold depth of spiritual grief. Despair is a deadly sin. If I
    have not yet committed it, it is only because my theoretic
    loyalty to the Vicar of Christ has deterred me. I tell you the
    truth, Pandulph, because I am a man of God and if God is
    not truth, God is nothing and my ministry is nothing. The
    fault of this King is that he has never understood the nature of
    truth. He has believed that it can be discovered in all worldly
    manifestations, whether good or bad, with no distinction
    made between them. It is as though he has looked through a
    painted church-window and said, 'Here the sky outside is
    red, here it is green, here it is yellow, and so forth.' Any man
    of any sense knows that the sky carries one colour only, its
    own colour, God's colour. God is not a glazier. Glaziers are
    arbitrary. So is the King.

PANDULPH. Yes. But if the King really thinks he sees all those
    colours, should not the men who have to deal with the king
    at least pretend to see them also? To continue your analogy –
    we put painted windows in our churches to educate and
    entertain the ignorant: but if we ourselves make too great a
    parade of our own private contempt for the secrets of the
    glazier's art, we are in danger of disillusioning our congre-
    gation.

MARSHAL. I am not altogether sure what you two gentlemen
    are talking about. But if the King does not confirm this
    Charter, the barons will depose him – they may even kill
    him. Untrustworthy or not, he is still the King of England
    and I have taken oaths in his service. Upon what does he
    stick? The Twenty-five Controllers? Would he accept them,
    do you think, if the barons were to renew their own old
    oaths of service and keep to those oaths?

ARCHBISHOP. I think that he might. But they have taken

C

many oaths in the past and they have broken them always.

MARSHAL. Under grave provocation. The King has continually demanded the shield-tax at times when no other king had ever been known to do so. We must be protected by precedent, Archbishop, there are certain precedents and customs governing the duties of the nobility of the realm, and here they are written down –

ARCHBISHOP. Yes, Marshal, yes. I am in agreement with you. Yes. But the King is not predictable. It is necessary to establish more than detailed precedent: we must set forward principles and make him keep to those. I am by no means convinced, Pandulph, that I have your support.

PANDULPH. The only principle which has my support, Your Grace – and it should be the only one to have yours – is the principle of the Supremacy of the Church in spiritual matters. Now the King, being a declared Crusader, has accepted that principle already.

MARSHAL. The King is no more a Crusader than I am a washer-woman. It is completely irrelevant to his quarrel with the barons.

PANDULPH. Do you think so? The leader of the barons has shewn no great love for the Church.

MARSHAL. Indeed, I fear not. Though he chooses to call himself the Marshal of the Army of God. Here he is now. I wonder what angel gives him his battle-orders? My Lord Fitzwalter . . .

> Enter FITZWALTER, DE VESCI, YOUNG MARSHAL *and other Barons, and the* MAYOR OF LONDON.
>
> FITZWALTER *acknowledges* MARSHAL'S *salutation with a nod.*

FITZWALTER. Ink, parchment, wax, black-beetles in attendance . . . He intends to put his seal? Or does he perhaps not so intend? Archiepiscopal embarrassment . . . Marshal, you have the air of a man whose nose has been tied to the tail of a dog. Where is he?

MARSHAL. The King, do you mean, sir?

FITZWALTER. His soldiers are in Flanders. Mine are across the river. Just over there. I shall allow him one hour. At the end of that time the Army of God will desire to eat its dinner.

ARCHBISHOP. It is unwise of you to call yourselves that.

DE VESCI. The Army of God? Justice belongs to God and we are hungry for justice.

ARCHBISHOP. Hungry. A just word. When your belly is full, the justice will be forgotten.

DE VESCI. I see no reason why you should insult your confederates in this rebellion. What articles of the Charter will the King not accept?

MARSHAL. Twenty-five over-kings to command the King of England.

FITZWALTER. That article is cardinal.

MARSHAL. I told him so. He will probably agree to it, if there is a second committee to help control the first.

FITZWALTER. He can have that if he wants. I will select it.

ARCHBISHOP. No sir. I will.

FITZWALTER. As you wish. What else?

ARCHBISHOP. The City of London. Whose liberties, you will remember, are to be affirmed in the Charter. Have you asked the Mayor if you may remain within his walls?

FITZWALTER. No, but I'll ask him now. May we, sir, remain within the walls of your city?

MAYOR. Why, you are there already, my Lord. I could not turn you out even if I wanted to. But I suppose you might say our liberties are much the same thing as yours, and your soldiers are needed to keep them. On a question of keeping – what about the king's promises, even if he does put his seal, do you think that he will?

YOUNG MARSHAL. Keep them? No sir.

MARSHAL. The word of your Sovereign is not to be disputed! I had not wished to speak to you. I do not recognize my son as a member of this rebellion.

YOUNG MARSHAL. If the King grants the Charter we will not be a rebellion. Our purposes are lawful, father.

MARSHAL. You have just said he will not grant it.

YOUNG MARSHAL. I said he will not keep to it.

MARSHAL. It is not for the son of the Marshal to doubt the honour of the King!

ARCHBISHOP. Gentlemen, at this present time, there is nothing that is not doubtful. Therefore, in order to shew the king that we at least have truth and justice for our cause, I would like you to subscribe to this small declaration I have concerned myself to draw up. Small but most important. (*He reads from a paper.*)

> 'Know that we are bound by oaths and homage to our Lord John King of England to protect faithfully his life limbs and worldly honour, against all mortal men, and to guard and defend his rights, the rights of his heirs, and the rights of his realm.'

My lord Robert Fitzwalter, will you put your seal on this? We can present it to the King.

FITZWALTER. No I will not. He must put his own seal on his own document first.

ARCHBISHOP. My Lord Eustace de Vesci?

DE VESCI. I have taken oaths to the King before. It is not necessary to repeat them.

ARCHBISHOP. It will help to convince the king that –

FITZWALTER (*drawing his sword*). His soldiers are in Flanders. Mine are across the river.

> *All the* BARONS *draw likewise (except* YOUNG MARSHAL.)

ARCHBISHOP. Is this your decisive answer?

FITZWALTER. Yes.

ARCHBISHOP. I am afraid that the King is not going to seal the Charter.

DE VESCI. We offered him one hour. It is not yet a quarter gone. We will wait.

> *The* BARONS *sit down, on the ground.*

ARCHBISHOP. Let me endeavour to persuade you once again –

FITZWALTER. No.

MARSHAL. Put away that sword, sir. It is most unseemly to draw your blades in the presence of your Marshal – when he has not drawn his.

DE VESCI. We are the Army of God and we have a Marshal of our own.

MARSHAL. You also have a Charter – there it is, written down, the Word of Law, sir, law, good precedent and good custom, the alternative to blood. Yet here you offer blood as the alternative to law, and I think you would prefer it.

FITZWALTER. Yes, I would too. This is John's Charter, not ours – he has foisted it upon us to withhold his own defeat and by God I do regret that ever we considered it!

ARCHBISHOP. No, Fitzwalter, no, it is not King John's Charter, it is derived from the Charter of King Henry I and according to ancient precedent. Your swords at this moment will devalue it completely. The Marshal is quite right.

FITZWALTER. The Marshal is too old, I have had enough of the Marshal, I am about to give the order to my army to set forward.

YOUNG MARSHAL. Your hour has not expired yet.

FITZWALTER. My hour expired last year. By further prolongation we are being made ridiculous.

> JOHN *enters, behind them, taking them by surprise. They automatically find themselves getting up, leaving their swords on the ground.*

JOHN. Indeed? Please be seated. Do you have the wax ready, Augustine? Good, to work then, to work.

> *The* CLERKS *begin to seal the Charter.*

> JOHN *sits down on the throne.*

Saucy Castle, which was built by my brother King Richard as the principal defence of Normandy, fell eleven years ago, through no fault of its commander: and, as a result, Normandy has ceased to be a possession of the English Crown. The reason why Saucy Castle was so easily captured has been explained as a mistake made by the engineer who planned it. The deep ditch which surrounded the central keep had one small ridge of rock left running across it. This acted as a shelter for King Philip's sappers and miners when they were engaged on the otherwise impossibly dangerous task of damaging the foundations of the great stone wall above. The wall collapsed in due course, and the garrison was, as they put it, reduced. As to why the ridge of rock had been left across the ditch, it would (I think) be unwise to accuse the engineers of any treacherous design. The plans of the castle were largely the work of my brother himself, who had not only no vested interest in the future loss of Normandy, but also was noted as the foremost exponent of the art of fortification in Christendom. Which all goes to shew, does it not, how fallible we are, and equally how fallible is likely to prove the work of our hands.

The sealed Charter is handed to him and he touches it.

This is the work of *my* hand, translate it into the proper formality, I Deliver this my Act and Deed, there you are, Fitzwalter, you may call off your dogs, we intend to hold a Council in the City of Oxford in the middle of next month, we shall be glad of your attendance.

He gets up abruptly and turns away. There is an awkward pause.

MARSHAL. The King has spoken, gentlemen.

FITZWALTER. Then there is no more to say. We will meet him at Oxford. In the meantime –

ARCHBISHOP. Copies will be sent at once to every corner of the kingdom. The Sheriffs of each County are to take order that it be read out aloud to the assembled population and displayed in the Cathedrals, so that all men will understand what has been agreed and what has been granted them, what Laws and what Customs have been established, and confirmed, and given under the King's Seal. At this forth-

coming Council, each article of the Charter will be exam-
ined in detail, and its immediate application conferred upon,
and enforced.

MARSHAL. The King gives you leave to depart. God Save the
King!

Some of the BARONS *sheepishly join in this invocation. The*
BARONS *and the* MAYOR *go out, awkwardly enough.*

JOHN. And you as well, William. Archbishop. Master
Pandulph. We are grateful for your duties, so freely carried
out . . . God's Bones, I am desirous to be left alone!

MARSHAL *and* ARCHBISHOP *go.* PANDULPH *retires to his*
chair, but does not sit down.

JOHN *addresses the* CLERKS.

You heard what the Archbishop said. See the document is
properly distributed from one end of England to the other.
He gave you a schedule, no doubt, of all the copies that are
to be made? Let me look at it . . . Yes, all these are correct . . .
And one additional copy, with an explanatory letter. Send
it to the Pope.

Exit JOHN.

PANDULPH *comes over to the* CLERK.

PANDULPH. You are astonished?

CLERK. There had been no provision made for a copy to the
Pope. But it will not take long to complete. Shall we sent it
to Rome, or commit it to you for despatch?

PANDULPH. The King told you to send it. It will get there so
much the quicker if you do.

CLERK. I suppose, when you come to think of it, sir, it is only
natural that His Holiness should be kept informed. After all –

PANDULPH. After all, the King is now his man. And all the
rebellions and coercive conspiracies that may take place
against the King, also in a sense take place against the person
of the Pope. For which reason his opinion concerning this
document may be said to be important. By the end of the
summer we in England should have heard it: and also by the

end of the summer the King should have had time to recruit
new troops in Flanders?

    As the CLERKS *busy themselves with the parchments,*
PANDULPH *comes downstage.*

Storm breaks in among the perfect circles,
Every day a puff of wind or a rumble of thunder
Declares some vain attempt to declare – what?
Very busy very busy very busy!
Whatever it is, it will be vain,
It will be some broken blunder:
But we who preserve the circles
Preserve their unfaulted music,
And we who are privileged to hear it
Can do no more than wonder
When presumptuous persons, particularly Bishops,
Believe that they with their own false notes can steer it
Into a new tune.
Why, they do not think that God speaks through their
                                          Charter?
This month is the twelve hundredth and fifteenth June
Since God *did* speak.
Who would dare to seek
For the marble fingers of Mount Sinai
Crooked around that serious young man's pen?
Blood bones and water
To be laughed at hereafter
Or brittle glass windows to be broken by broken men.

    He rolls up his chart and goes.

Act Two

SCENE ONE

A sealed copy of the Charter hung opposite PANDULPH'*s chair.
A picture of the interior of a Gothic building of some complexity,
with clerks sitting writing at desks.*

Enter PANDULPH *and* CLERK – *the latter carrying an armful
of parchments.*

PANDULPH. Very busy very busy, yes.

CLERK. Do you think it necessary for copies of these to be
sent to the Pope?

PANDULPH. I doubt it. His Holiness has been told about the
sow – he ought to be able to deduce the piglets, surely?

CLERK (*shewing him the parchments*). Chancery Writs for the
most part, dealing with various personal grievances which
come within the general terms of the Charter. For example,
many noblemen have long claimed in vain the possession of
castles which the King has sequestered for non-payment of
debt or for failure in loyalty, or, you might say, for no
reason at all – a simple expression of royal disfavour. They
are now to be told that the King's action was not in accordance with the Ancient Laws and Customs: and they may
have their castles back. Thus the Lord de Quenci obtains
Mountsorrel Castle, the Lord Fitzallen Richmond Castle,
and the Lord Fitzwalter – to whom I would personally grant
no more than a six-foot trench of earth – is awarded the
custody of the castle of Hereford. Eustace de Vesci – to
whom I would personally grant no more than a six-foot
trench of earth with quick-lime in it – is permitted once
again to resume his traditional hunting rights in the County
of Durham. May he catch a rabbit that has eaten some un-
wholesome herb and die of it himself. Of course there is no

question but that the King has acted in the past, one might say, illegally. Why not? When unscrupulous men were using the forms of legality to withhold justice, to oppress their people, and to refuse their dutiful services to the household of their sovereign? Why not?

PANDULPH. For the King to amend his own inequitable judgements is a praiseworthy work. But all the judgements he has given are not now accounted inequitable, are they?

CLERK. No, indeed, why should they?

PANDULPH. And he is not yet an old man. Or at least he would not be if he disciplined his appetites. He has many more judgements to give. Can he give them, do you think, from his own free heart and mind as a son of his father anointed by the Oil of God, when twenty-five disloyal barons, unanointed, chosen only by their own self-evident partial word, are to superintend his every act?

CLERK. They can, I suppose, ensure that the King's proceedings do not go too far counter to the promises made at Runnymede – if the King conducts their conduct as carefully as he knows how, they need perhaps no more impede him than ministers or advisers commonly do. Which has not in the past been a very extensive impediment, shall we say?

PANDULPH. In the past maybe, no. But now you will find it different: for these men are pragmatic, they are arbitrary and unpredictable. Of course the King has been accused of being exactly the same himself. But Our Lord once compared the Kingdom of Heaven to an unjust judge: He also told a story of most unsuitable wages offered by an overseer for work in a vineyard, and told it what is more with apparent approval. The afflictions of Job came upon him for no reason; and when the Tower of Siloam fell, the men who were killed by it were in no way outrageous sinners above all who dwelt in Israel. God, by definition, cannot be unjust: therefore, these apparent inequities, when related to the whole of the Divine Wisdom which we are not yet able to perceive, will prove to be by no means as arbitrary as they may seem. Such examples, however, though they may justify the King, can never do so for the barons. Their committee of twenty-five is set up without sanction: it condemns its own self: and you will find it a stumbling-block.

CLERK. Sir, you underestimate the King. He has not yet met the twenty-five. When the Council at Oxford commences –
Enter JOHN.

JOHN – I think we shall be horrified by some indecent exposure . . . Pandulph, do not dare to say to your most venerable master that I am not an honest man. (*He indicates the parchments.*) Look at all these – silver and gold buttons, jewelled hooks and eyes, snipped from my own garments, my own most personal underwear, and tossed to the disgusting multitude, broadcast largesse like a king in a fairy tale – and for what reason sir? Because I gave my word. My conscience is clear when I enter this Council. I am in process already of abiding by the Charter. But will they be?

Aha, we shall discover.
By the look upon their faces
And their posture in their places,
We shall know what they intend.
God defend
But that I should prove
An easy man to love:
But if hatred is their preference
My own posture at this conference
Will be that of a very hedgehog!

Are we ready, Augustine, are the Barons in Council assembled? Shall we go in?

CLERK. Yes, Your Grace, the Barons attend upon you.

JOHN. The tone of your voice – not very confident . . . why not? Never mind. To business, to business . . .

PANDULPH *sits down in his chair. The Council is dis-*

covered – a throne in the centre, two benches for the Coun-
cillors flanking it. These are occupied by all the BARONS
from Act I, MARSHAL *and the* ARCHBISHOP.
When they see the KING, *the* MARSHAL *and* ARCHBISHOP
rise. The others remain seated.

MARSHAL. My lords, the King's Grace, my lords!

JOHN. Thank you, William: but I have been observed, I think. Gentlemen, we are making our entrance. Do you not intend to rise, as a sign of your respect? . . . Very well, you may be seated. So their postures are relaxed, are they?

He goes and stands by the throne.

A relaxed posture is good for the digestion, I am told. No doubt you have dined heavily. I am suffering from gout, and my doctor has not yet allowed me to eat anything today except for one inconsiderable collation. I am therefore hungry, impatient, somewhat irritable, and quite happy to stand. Despite the pain in my foot. In my right foot, extreme pain. This Council is declared to be in session, and as I look at this Council, in session, indeed, as I walk up and down the hall in which this Council is contained – (*He walks up and down*) – I come rapidly to the conclusion that there is only one thing to discuss. Any examination of the detailed provision of the Charter is entirely redundant, until you remove your troops from the City of London. Your side of the agreement, you equivocating whoremongers – are you going to keep to it or not!

DE VESCI (*leaping to his feet*). Don't you call me a whore-monger – there are known facts against you –

FITZWALTER (*ditto*). Insults and abuse is not what we have come here for –

Other BARONS *jump up, shouting –*

BARONS (*generally*). Abide by the Charter – Fulfil your promises – Why don't you keep your word – etc. etc.

JOHN. Good, you're on your feet. Then I can relieve mine, at

the expense of my buttocks – the gout hasn't reached those
I'm glad to say.

He sits down on the throne. The BARONS *are not quite*
decided whether to stand or sit.

Eustace, now you're up there, you can stay up! You too,
Fitzwalter! That's better . . . Now will you all please sit. So,
having re-established the normal courtesies, let us hear
about these 'known facts'. A little lubricious scandal always
helps to oil the wheels of government. At least when *I'm*
turning the crankshaft it does . . . Go on. then, my bold
cock-a-doodle-dandy – facts, if you please, boy, facts!

DE VESCI. I am a man of unimpeachable nobility. My ancestors –

JOHN. We are not here concerned with your ancestors,
Eustace. We want facts – against *me* – remember?

DE VESCI. You have seduced, contrary to all the regulations of
polite conduct, and the accepted order of society, you have
seduced –

JOHN. Her, her, and her . . . at different intervals of time, and
with different degrees of pleasure. Yes. So have you. Does it
matter?

DE VESCI. I am alluding to ladies of established parentage. I
am alluding to ladies of established matrimonial status. I am
alluding to –

JOHN. You are alluding to your own wife, Eustace – and taking
a very long time to come to the point. So it does matter. She
was yours, and I took her. Have you proof?

DE VESCI. My lords, this is intolerable!

JOHN. It would be, if you had proof, beyond her own word for
it, and women will say anything. So will some men. You
know where the proof will lie – it will lie in the accounts of
the Royal Exchequer, because you know very well that if I
did take your wife it would have been because you yourself
desired me to remit you your taxes. Justifiable taxes. The

King is short of money and will do anything to get it – which is why we are here today. The money is demanded in lieu of levied soldiers, the wife is demanded in lieu of levied money. You don't imagine that an ugly old wineskin like me seduced her by the exercise of my physical charms, do you? God corrode my sweetbreads, de Vesci, did she come to me for nothing! Or did she never come at all? We will not discuss the question of prostitution any further. I mentioned the City of London, I want an answer.

ARCHBISHOP. My Lord –

JOHN. I was really addressing the Marshal of the Army of God, my Lord, who has not yet opened his mouth – at least to any purpose. However, God has another army, happily celibate. You may speak.

ARCHBISHOP. The barons have refused to leave London, my Lord.

JOHN. Why?

ARCHBISHOP. They have a reason. It is not a very good one, in my opinion: but as military men, they justify it thus. Until it becomes manifest that the royal obligations contained in the Charter are to be adhered to, they do not see why they should be compelled to remove a garrison which, again from the point of view of military men, affords them great advantage.

JOHN. So it does. They sit down in London, and they sit down in my Council, and they leave it to me to weary my poor afflicted legs. I know why they sit in London. If they want help from the King of France, all he has to do is to sail up the Thames to them. Which makes them feel so strong they can defy their King to his face, their conciliatory benevolent King, who seeks only to make peace with them. It is absolutely unheard-of that subjects under allegiance can remain seated upon the entry of their monarch: and the only thing that makes them rise is obscenities in the mouth of that monarch. We are amazed . . . Archbishop, if I could

kill these fellows here, I would. But at the moment I can't.
Can you suggest an alternative?

ARCHBISHOP. Temperance.

JOHN. God help us – for whom?

ARCHBISHOP. For everyone, sire. In order to offer aid to the
army in London, any French expedition must somehow
pass the Tower. Now, if the Tower were held –

JOHN. By the King? It would be wonderful. But I don't hold
it, so why mention it?

ARCHBISHOP. Not by the King, my lord. By me.

JOHN. I was not aware that you were in the possession of
troops.

ARCHBISHOP. The Tower garrison is a permanent one,
allegedly in your service. But the Constable there has
declared for the barons. If he has changed sides once, he can
change them again. My Lord Fitzwalter, will you allow this
officer to put himself under my orders?

DE VESCI. Can you trust him?

ARCHBISHOP. Can you?

DE VESCI. The Tower is generally recognized as impregnable.
So in fact, if he chooses, the fellow inside of it can have the
laugh on all of us.

FITZWALTER. We're not giving up the Tower – Holy Virgin,
it is impregnable!

DE VESCI. So long as we have an army in London town itself,
I think we can give it up.

A BARON. We're not giving up the Tower.

DE VESCI (*beckoning* FITZWALTER *and some others into a
huddle*). Come here . . . the Constable at present is our man.
There is no doubt about that. Therefore it will do us no
harm if he puts himself under the orders of the Archbishop –
as a diplomatic fiction, for God's sake. The Constable is not
going to stand all-alone-except-for-Jesus at the corner of the
city when we occupy the rest of it. (*He jerks his thumb at the*
ARCHBISHOP.) *He* can do that sort of thing any time he

wants, he's three-quarters of a saint, isn't he? – it's his business. The Constable is a soldier, the business of a soldier is to be on the side that wins, which is either us or King Slapstick, it is certainly not Canterbury. Have I made myself clear? (*He rejoins the main body of the Council.*) My Lord of Canterbury, in the interests of peace, the Army of God is glad to accord to the Clergy of God permission to hold the Tower.

ARCHBISHOP. My Lord Fitzwalter?

FITZWALTER. Eh? Yes, of course, your permission is accorded. Did you not hear him say so?

ARCHBISHOP. Thank you, my Lord.

JOHN. Peace will no doubt be grateful for your concern for her interests, Eustace. She is represented, I believe, in antique statuary, as a beautiful woman, dishevelled, subject to occasional rape. And how long, Archbishop, do you propose to occupy my castle, upon your own volition, while my city next door to it is occupied by these, upon their own volition?

ARCHBISHOP. As a temporary compromise only, my Lord.

JOHN. Then put a term to it, sir.

ARCHBISHOP. The Feast of the Assumption?

FITZWALTER. When is that?

ARCHBISHOP. Really, my Lord . . .

JOHN. Well, when is it? We are not the Diocesan Chapter, you know. (*To* CLERK.) Do you know when is it?

CLERK. The fifteenth of August, my Lord.

JOHN. One month. Very good. You're out of London in one month. Agreed?

FITZWALTER. This can be agreed, yes –
     DE VISCI *whispers in his ear.*
That is to say, provided –

JOHN. Provided what? That the King of France brings in one thousand archers?

FITZWALTER. No. That the King of England brings in none

at all; and that all the nobility, the chief clerisy, the judiciary, in fact the entire apparatus of this kingdom, have taken oaths to accept the Charter. They have not yet done so. Furthermore, they must obey the Charter and in particular the newly-established Council of Twenty-five Barons as represented here. It must be understood that we are the Kingdom of England!

JOHN. God help the English.

> JOHN *goes out abruptly.*
>
> *After a moment's confusion the Council disperses, everyone leaving the stage (including* PANDULPH), *except the* CLERK, *who remains, sorting out his parchments.*
>
> JOHN *re-enters with the* ARCHBISHOP *and* MARSHAL.

JOHN. Augustine, shew to these disturbed dignitaries the work you have in hand.

CLERK. These are but a few, my lords, among the enormous number of documents which scriveners of the Household are hastening to complete. They are at their desks night and day –

ARCHBISHOP. Very probably. I have no desire to examine the parchments. If the King states that the provisions of the Charter are being carried out by his servants, it is not for me to put his word to the test. Sire, why did you not declare these letters to the Council? It might have helped to mollify –

JOHN. If you do not presume to put my word to the test, why should they? My word was given at Runnymede: surely I have no need to repeat it.

MARSHAL. All that they require, sire, is an earnest of good faith.

JOHN. Our Seal is upon the Charter, Marshal. Is not that sufficient?

MARSHAL. Sire, I will speak boldly –

JOHN. Will you? You sound overwhelmed by the force of your own intention; I do not know why. There has been, if anything, an excess of bold speaking today. However, do

D

not let yourself be inhibited by your tardy recognition of the atmosphere of the time. Continue, be bold. Sit down, if you wish, and extend your feet before me, omit nothing that will proclaim you to be a man of the mode.

MARSHAL. The mode, sire, disgusts me. But it is a mode that derives from prolonged suspicion and frustration upon both sides of the argument. The barons are aware that although much of the Charter is no more than a recapitulation of previous Charters, – King Henry I, I believe –

ARCHBISHOP. That is correct. King Henry II also made various undertakings, which –

MARSHAL. Quite so. But there is no precedent for the imposition upon the King of the twenty-five Lords Commissioner, or whatever they call themselves. There has always of course been a Council of State to offer advice and it has generally been to the advantage of the commonwealth that such advice should be respected on the part of the King. But a Council with power to forbid a royal enactment – indeed to forbid it under the threat of armed rebellion, which is what the Charter provides for, my Lord Archbishop, and I told you at the time it should never have been framed in precisely those terms –

JOHN. Keep to the point, sir, the whole damned thing should never have been framed . . .

MARSHAL. Such a Council is most dangerous and the more dangerous indeed for being unrepresentative in its members. Had a Parliament been chosen from among *all* your nobility instead of merely from the partisans of Fitzwalter and de Vesci, then perhaps – but in any case, sire: they know as well as we do that their demands are exorbitant, that you cannot be expected to lie down beneath them, and that – well, they are afraid of your reaction and hence behave so badly. I have tried to excuse them: but their conduct is unpardonable, and it's no use trying to blink it.

JOHN. I do not try to blink it – as you have seen.

ARCHBISHOP. I *have* seen it, sire, with abundant sorrow. Surely it is obvious that a promise of liberty is worth nothing to the liberated unless it can be enforced?

JOHN. Archbishop, it is a promise that has been given by your King!

ARCHBISHOP. As the Marshal has just reminded us, you are not the first King to have been compelled to give it.

JOHN. Indeed sir, I am, the very first indeed, to have been *compelled*.

ARCHBISHOP. Which only makes it worse. History demonstrates and you have admitted that kings have broken faith. It is sheer minstrelcraft and rhetoric to pretend otherwise, and I for one am not impressed by it.

MARSHAL. *My* Lord, please, be careful –

ARCHBISHOP. No I will not. I am not now a subject appealing to his king, I am a priest of the Lord God reproaching a devious man! John, son of Henry, the truth in you has been found wanting, too many times.

JOHN (*for a moment it seems as though he is going to strike him*). Stephen son of – I don't know who your father was and I am surprised you think it appropriate to mention the name of mine. He too had difficulties with one of his Archbishops. It was more than a word that was broken upon that occasion, I remember.

ARCHBISHOP. Words, bones, and hearts – all of them are fragile. *My* heart, what about it? (*He points to the Charter.*) That work on the wall is the blood of my heart and if in defence of it I do have to suffer the fate of Thomas Becket I will not turn my hand to the abatement of its meaning! . . . But this is foolish, I am sorry, I have only this moment described your method of speech as minstrelcraft; and here I am parading my own swollen words like any Lancelot or Roland in an unreliable romance.

JOHN. Don't be ashamed of yourself, we all enjoy poetry. My brother Richard Lionheart even used to compose it, and

when he was taken prisoner it was his minstrel who discovered where – unfortunately . . .

ARCHBISHOP. But the poetry that will arise from this cap-
tivity will not be enjoyable. For who can take pleasure when
virtue is in a dungeon and there are none to bring her out?
Yet such will be the song, the lament that will survive you.
It is not only yourself whose sovereignty is committed to
the Charter – your little son Henry, when he becomes king,
and his son, if he has one, and so on into the future to your
uttermost posterity – all these kings and queens will govern
according to custom and justice as set out in that schedule:
or else it is most unlikely that they will ever govern at all.

MARSHAL. Archbishop, this sounds like treason. If they do
not govern, who will?

ARCHBISHOP. The truth, not only of John, but of the House
of Plantagenet, will have been weighed in the balances,
Marshal, and found wanting altogether – Mene, mene tekel
'upharsin' – their inheritance shall be given over to the Medes
and to the Persians – it is written, upon the wall!

Exit ARCHBISHOP, *weeping.*

JOHN. I suppose he means the French. Is it possible he could
be in league with them and be designing they should invade
this country? Was I unwise perhaps to allow him to command the Tower of London?

MARSHAL. Sire, I cannot believe that –

JOHN. I have always regarded him as honest. But he is a
cleric – consider his history – he is trained to wear two faces.
Here he is again.

The ARCHBISHOP *re-enters.*

MARSHAL (*to* CLERK). What is his history?

CLERK. University of Paris. Scholastic theology.

JOHN. Hardly a hopeful cradle for simply saintly pastors . . .
Well, sir, have you returned? You need not have troubled –
I heard no-one cry 'encore'.

ARCHBISHOP. I am the man responsible for the Charter: I am

the man who persuaded the barons to select from among
their multifarious demands only those that could be justified
by reference to ancient custom, and to cast away so many
others that were selfish and tyrannous. The matter of the
twenty-five, I grant you, was clumsily handled: but there
had to be something like it, enforcement was essential. I am
the man who codified and condensed certain broad, and in
my opinion unwise, generalizations which you yourself, sire,
suggested – I mean those clauses relating to the refusal of
justice and imprisonment without trial. The principle
behind them was good, but I think the barons would have
preferred them in a more specific form, and I had enough
trouble as it was to keep the barons contented, without
inserting articles that might one day affect their own private
privilege. I am, in fact, the man who has brought the liberty
of the subject and the prerogative of the crown to march a
little inwards from their palisaded lines, till both have been
able to meet, here, on the parchment, in what might have
been the place of darkest slaughter in the midst of a stricken
field. Is my hard employment, then, to be so readily
rejected?

JOHN. No, Stephen, no, it is not. We know you to be a true
man, indeed, the truth of Jesus Christ is evident in your
mouth – and despite our light and scornful disposition, we
can never reject that. Please remember in mitigation that the
House of Plantagenet is supposed to be descended from the
Devil – we are Christians now, but not always very good
ones. Nevertheless, I still do not see how I am going to be
able to trust –

MARSHAL. Sire, I will speak boldly, and if you please, this
time, do not jeer at me until you have heard me out. When
your great predecessor King Arthur found himself at war
with Mordred his unhappy son – yes indeed, it is minstrelcraft; but the deeds of the Round Table are an example to
all good knights today. Arthur and Mordred brought their

armies together on the field of Camlann. With difficulty a
trumpet-of-parley was secured, and negotiations began
between the chiefs. But alas, a little adder, creeping out of
a bracken-bush, came up to one of the King's knights and
stung him on the ankle. The knight drew his sword to cut
the serpent in two, the drawn sword was observed by the
armies on either hand, they took for granted there was
treachery at work, and battle was immediately joined, with
appalling ferocity. Two men alone survived from that
conflict. The King was not one of them.

JOHN. But you were, I suppose. Forgive my frivolity, William;
I am as much moved by your plea as by the steadfastness
of the Archbishop. If I were to weep in front of you, no
doubt you would call me crocodile. Answer me one question.
How can I induce the barons to return to their castles?
Even had I shewed them proofs of all the vast administration
I have been conducting for their benefit, I still do not
believe that they would stir their stumps and go. They will
be in London long after the Feast of the Assumption. Will
they not? Of course they will, and you know it. What are
they afraid of, that they keep their army together so long?

MARSHAL. Your own army of Flemings, sire, when you bring
them across the Channel.

JOHN. I have no intention whatever of bringing Flemings
across the Channel.

ARCHBISHOP. Sire, is that true?

JOHN. Of course it is true. I am not an idiot, Archbishop. I too
prefer even a humiliating charter to continued civil war.

MARSHAL. Sire, this is very important. The barons clearly
believe that you are recruiting soldiers in Flanders. If I can,
in your name, assure them that you are not, I think there is
an excellent chance that they will evacuate London.

JOHN. You do? Very well. So listen to this. We are graciously
pleased to afford you that assurance, as solemnly as we may.
We only desire to levy soldiers from those who have a duty

to supply them: in other words, our loyal barons. Good God,
sir, you do not need me to tell you, the mercenary armies of
Flanders are notorious for uncontrolled brutality, and we
shall be glad to be rid of their help – if it can be so described.
Augustine, write at once to all the recruiting agents in the
Low Countries, with whom we may in past time have been
in communication, and tell them we have no further need
of their services. Write the letters today and let the Marshal
read them through before they are despatched. Sufficient?
Very good.

    Exeunt JOHN *and* CLERK.

ARCHBISHOP. The army in London must be disbanded. This
    could be a way to do it. I can conceive of no other.

MARSHAL. I am the one to carry this to the barons. If the King
    is dishonourable, my name will be marked with the blotch.
    Thus I fulfil my duty to the son of Henry Curtmantle and
    to the brother of the Lionheart.

    Exit MARSHAL.

    The ARCHBISHOP *is on the way out by a different door,
    when he is met by* PANDULPH *coming in.*

PANDULPH. My Lord, I have often heard His Holiness, when
    reminiscent after the evening meal with a few dear com-
    panions, refer affectionately to the days that you and he
    spent together at the University in Paris.

ARCHBISHOP. I am rejoiced that the Holy Father should so
    remember me.

PANDULPH. He has spoken more than once of a course of
    lectures you gave upon the Duties of the Episcopal Office.

ARCHBISHOP. They did achieve some small celebrity, in their
    theoretic way. But as a guide to the present insensate pre-
    dicament, I do not recommend you to study them.

PANDULPH. Did you have anything to say to your students
    about the conduct of a bishop in command of a metropolitan
    fortress?

ARCHBISHOP. No.

PANDULPH. Not even when the surrounding city is held by a potentially hostile army?

Exit ARCHBISHOP.

Every additional closely-written line
That tries to fix, determine, and define,
Instead of a hard bright link in an irremovable chain,
Becomes rather the blade of a new hard wedge
Sledged into the tree-trunk to split the protesting grain.

Enter CLERK, *with a letter.*

And here comes one of the hammers.

CLERK. This letter, sir, is addressed by the King to a gentle-man of the name of Hugh de Boves, last known to be resident in the City of Bruges. He is a contractor for the supply of mercenary soldiers: and will, for a due profit, raise, equip, and transport entire armies to wherever they may be in demand. The population of the Low Countries is at present excessive, so he makes a good living.

PANDULPH. He will make a better one in hell, after he is dead.

CLERK. Precisely so. There is, I believe, a special bailiewick in the Pit of Lucifer laid apart for stirrers-up of strife . . . Now, the King is about to send another letter to Sir Hugh to tell him he has decided to cancel the contract that was negotiated last month. *This* letter will contradict that letter and for obvious reasons cannot be sent openly. Therefore the King would be exceedingly grateful if you, being the Papal Representative, and therefore, one might say, above suspicion, could personally take charge of this and despatch it by your own messenger.

PANDULPH *takes the letter and looks at it dubiously.*

You need not be afraid, it is written in cipher. This may appear villainous on the part of the King, but whatever the hopes of the Archbishop, he is certain in his mind that the leaders of the barons no longer regard the Charter as a satisfactory solution to their various grievances.

PANDULPH. Do they not? Do they not? Then what more do they want?

CLERK. As much as they can take, until the King dies and he is succeeded by a nine-year-old child – and then who will govern England?

PANDULPH. I hope not Sir Hugh de Boves . . . Nevertheless, I will deliver the letter.

CLERK. The King will be most grateful.

Exeunt severally.

SCENE TWO

A view of London river with the Bridge and the Tower.
A table and stools. On the table, wine and flagons, with a dicebox.
Enter DE VESCI, pours himself a drink, drinks, and plays dice, muttering profanities.
LADY DE VESCI enters.

DE VESCI. I was under the impression, madam, I had ordered you to remain in this lodging. I have just returned from Oxford, you were not here when I came back. Where were you?

LADY DE VESCI. I walked abroad to see the city, my Lord. What is so remarkable about that? The citizens' wives do it every day.

DE VESCI. Very possibly, madam. They have not been forbidden it by their husbands. You have.

LADY DE VESCI. I would be glad to hear the reason.

DE VESCI. You know very well the reason. I will not sully my mouth by repeating it. Why, you are nothing but a navigable river, a sluice, madam.

LADY DE VESCI. Continue.

DE VESCI. What do you mean, continue? I am waiting to hear you defend yourself. Will you please defend yourself, madam!

LADY DE VESCI. It should be easier for you to prove that I have been the King's mistress than for me to prove that I have not.

DE VESCI. I could put you in prison for what you have done to my honour – have you flogged by my knaves. It would not in any way be regarded as outrageous.

LADY DE VESCI. By the terms of the Charter which the King has just granted you, I think it might be regarded as extremely outrageous.

DE VESCI. The Charter, what Charter? It has nothing to do with you!

LADY DE VESCI (*reading from the Charter*). 'No free man shall be arrested or imprisoned or deprived of his freehold . . . except by the lawful judgement of his peers'. I am a free woman, indeed, a noblewoman – if you can establish a court of noble ladies of equivalent rank, I daresay they will be prepared to hear your cause against me, and to pronounce a verdict in accordance with the evidence.

DE VESCI. Evidence – why, I have enough evidence –

LADY DE VESCI. Nonsense, you have none.

DE VESCI. None. Except what is sung at every street corner and whispered in every corridor of every castle in the land . . . and what in the name of the Black Blood of Mahound do you mean by putting that sort of interpretation upon a document which – which does not mean what you think it means. No. The clause that you so amused yourself by quoting at your husband, at your Lord, was specifically intended to prevent men of my class from being hauled before tribunals consisting of persons of inferior rank – commoners and foreigners and God knows who besides. You know very well what the King's been doing with his Law-Courts – French clerks, and so forth, mercenary officers, he has had the impertinence to describe them as his Judges – well, he on't do it any more, we've put the cork in that bottle! And not in such a way as to give free passage for adultery, I hope.

LADY DE VESCI. Adultery with the King.

DE VESCI. He will not protect you here. We are in London now, and fortified.

LADY DE VESCI. Which is more than your Charter is, I'm afraid!

DE VESCI. I do not understand you.

LADY DE VESCI. The interpretation I put upon that clause may well have been unusual, though a lady in danger must grasp at any weapon:

When pursued by strong conquerors
We cannot be pickers and choosers.
For Cleopatra there was a small brown serpent,
For Daphne a green tree:
Sappho, I remember, jumped into the sea,
Penelope with her loom imposed on lechery constraint,
Jezebel spread out her pots of raddle and paint
And her stiff embroidered raiment:
Judith was fortunate – she had a sword.
All that is left for me
Is an ambidextrous word
Scrawled upon dry parchment.
Why should I care if you think it impertinent?

DE VESCI. Ambidextrous, ambidextrous, you say that of a word? A word means what it says and what it is meant to say – are you trying to tell me it can mean anything you want it to mean? Why, if this were found to be true –

LADY DE VESCI. Well, my Lord, if –

Enter FITZWALTER (*shewn in by a* SERVANT).

He helps himself to a drink.

FITZWALTER. The Mayor of London is in the courtyard with a face like a belt-buckle. He wishes to speak to us.

DE VESCI. He can wait. Something has just struck my mind, Robert – you may go, madam – struck it very forcibly –

FITZWALTER. Young Marshal has completed the arrangements for the tournament. We can hold it out at Hounslow, there is a good wide field, and the carpenters have had orders to put the stands up directly. (*He throws a dice and looks at the numbers.*)

Five and a four.

Nine green girls in a dancing line.

Are you going to have a throw?

DE VESCI. The words of the Charter – it has occurred to me suddenly that they are liable to misconstruction.

FITZWALTER. Very probably they are – are you going to throw the dice or not? A word is a word, you can turn it inside out like an old coat as many times as you want to; but victory in war, Eustace, is alone irreversible. Throw if you please.

DE VESCI *throws*. FITZWALTER *checks the score*.

Three and a five

Dead men eight have met their fate.

DE VESCI *passes a coin over*.

Thank you.

DE VESCI. Of course, you are quite right, there is no reason why *we* should be concerned about words . . . What about this war anyway? The old Marshal has solemnly informed me that Landless John has decided to dispense with his landless army. He has written letters to Flanders to say – send no more mercenaries. Are we to believe him?

FITZWALTER. We cannot but believe the old Marshal, he is the very shield and helm of rectitude – but for all that, he is a good man, I was a page in his household when I was a boy, he is an honest man: so therefore the news is true. But whether John's letters are true is quite another matter. Maybe they are. I think he is frightened. He knows that our own recruitment in the northern counties is increasing every week. He does not want a war. It will be very expensive and there is a strong chance he will lose it. (*He throws the dice.*)

DE VESCI (*counting them*).

Three and a two

Five wounds of blood on the Holy Cross of God.

I can do better than that. So, if there is not a war – and it *will* be expensive, I had rather do without it myself – we are committed to a Charter: and, as I have told you already, I am not at all sure that I know what it means.

FITZWALTER. I think we are going to be able to put upon that Charter whatever interpretation we think best. You ought not to be so scrupulous.

DE VESCI. No, I am not scrupulous. I am far-sighted if you like. (*Plays and looks at dice.*)

One, and bloody one

Tiny two, how do you do –

No, I am *not* paying up on that one, my attention was distracted.

LADY DE VESCI. It isn't a game of skill.

DE VESCI. What! Are you still here?

LADY DE VESCI. You can't plead distraction over dice. It is not the same thing as conversation with a lady. If it were, I am sure we would all be most happy to remit you your forfeits, otherwise you would be bankrupt.

DE VESCI. I shall remember this.

FITZWALTER. Which reminds me, young Marshal wants a lady, to be the Queen of Love at the tournament. Whose name should we put forward?

DE VESCI. We don't need a Queen of Love – I thought the purpose of a tournament was to fit ourselves for battle.

FITZWALTER. So it is, but apparently these things are done in Provence and young Marshal thinks he should introduce them here. It will entertain the citizens, and to judge from the expression upon the Mayor's countenance this evening – he is below stairs, I told you – they are in need of entertainment. I suggested your own wife. Have you any objections?

DE VESCI. Are you trying to insult me?

FITZWALTER. It would help you to demonstrate in public that you are not concerned for what was said to you at Oxford. You should take pains to indicate that the lady was seduced against her will and that you bear her no malice for it.

DE VESCI. For what possible reason do you imagine I should bear her no malice?

FITZWALTER. Christian charity. We have the Archbishop to think of, Eustace. If the Archbishop is not with us, I am afraid we will have lost the Mayor of London too. It is necessary for us to be more than a mere faction – I have said so many times.

LADY DE VESCI. I think you had better understand, my Lord Robert, I intend to preside over no tournament, whether for reasons of politics or personal reconciliation.

DE VESCI. She was ordered to go to her private apartment.

FITZWALTER. And yet she defies you. Why don't you take your belt to her?

DE VESCI. Oh yes, I did once, yes, and what happened? You saw very well what happened, at the Council at Oxford. She is encouraged by these damned garlic-mouth poets, there was a herd of them associated with the old black witchcraft queen – you know who I am talking about – Aquitanian Eleanor – *his* mother, that's the one – she brought them into Normandy and then into England, till we don't know where we stand. The fit and proper order laid out in good numbers, one–two–three–four–five it used to be, and no-one contradicted, but it's all over the map of Europe now, five–two–four–three–one or four–two–three–one–five, knees between the elbows and head between the ankles, that's custom and morality today! Seven Devils inside of Maudlin – she's still here and she's grinning – Blood of the Martyrs, Gabriel's Golden Gap, will you go to your room this minute – !

He grabs his wife and throws her down in fury, then starts dragging her impotently about the stage. FITZWALTER *gives way to laughter.*

Enter YOUNG MARSHAL.

YOUNG MARSHAL. Oh . . . I had not intended . . .

FITZWALTER. She won't go to her room. And he can't get her to go to her room. By God I have seen a Lombard crossbow serjeant keep better discipline upon a strumpet of the camp.

DE VESCI (*leaving her and turning upon* YOUNG MARSHAL). I have a sufficiency of servants: why could they not announce you?

FITZWALTER. This is indelicate of you, boy. I hope you are ashamed.

YOUNG MARSHAL. I ask your pardon, Eustace, if I had known I would have . . . but I have had a message today – from my father's chaplain – my father himself will have nothing to do with me – he tells me that the King has written letters to Flanders –

FITZWALTER. Yes we know, we have heard it.

YOUNG MARSHAL. Then should we not disband our army at once? It is also a fact that Writs have been issued from the Royal Chancery confirming all the liberties that were granted in the Charter.

DE VESCI. All of them?

YOUNG MARSHAL. Most of them.

DE VESCI. It will have to be all of them. And they must all pass inspection. There is too much latitude in that Charter. I am highly suspicious of it.

FITZWALTER (*to* YOUNG MARSHAL). I thought that we commissioned you to provide us with some diversion this evening? Three strong whores from Billingsgate were spoken of, I believe.

YOUNG MARSHAL (*looking at the lady*). Surely under the circumstances it would be a failure of courtesy to –

DE VESCI. Bring them up, boy. At once! You may oppose your

father in politics, but you have yet over-many of his inherited
cobwebs making dismal your social habit. We'll have 'em
up, make haste, make haste, young Galahad.

> YOUNG MARSHAL *goes out with an embarrassed bob to the*
> *Lady, to whom* DE VESCI *now addresses himself.*

Do you still intend to remain in this apartment?

FITZWALTER. What about the Mayor – we are keeping him
waiting?

DE VESCI. He may join us if he wishes . . . Pray be seated,
madam, do not on any account put yourself to inconvenience
by absenting yourself from our pastime.

> YOUNG MARSHAL *re-enters with three* GIRLS (*one blonde,*
> *one dark, and one red-haired*).

YOUNG MARSHAL. Ladies, the Lord Fitzwalter; the Lord de
Vesci, whose lodging this is; the Lord de Vesci's –

DE VESCI. Good, let us adjust ourselves. You, you're for this
gentleman. Robert, this one's yours: this one (*the blonde*)
because she's the fattest, she's a great big pig is this one, *I*
am going to take. What's your name, you lovely porker –
never mind, no names at all is better, you give no-one your
name and they can't put a witchcraft on you: so I intend to
baptize you all with names of my own choosing and by these
names you shall be known until morning.

> *The* GIRLS *sit down, professionally, and start in on wine and*
> *spices.*

> DE VESCI *walks round them, appraising them.*

Deadly Nightshade:

Which grows in the dark recesses of the wood:

Serve it to your good friends: they need no further food.

Red Herring:

The dogs in full cry get this one up their nose.

Free may run the quick vixen and the dun deer and his does.

Chop-chop-and-chew-it:

Hot bacon grease runs out of the old man's mouth,

Vinegar settles his stomach, it will never quench his drouth.

Very good. They tell me King Arthur would never drive his teeth into his dinner without he had first heard some wonderful new thing. We'll follow his example. The son of the Marshal is going to sing us a song. A song of the South of France, boy, for the benefit of milady, who would no doubt prefer to be there.

YOUNG MARSHAL. I will attempt one, Eustace, if you wish. For the benefit of my lady, if she will accept it.

LADY DE VESCI. Why yes, she will, why not?

YOUNG MARSHAL (*sings*).

> I send my song to one who cannot hear it:
> In no green garden does her beauty stroll.
> I send a robe of gold, she cannot wear it:
> In bitter sackcloth she her limbs must roll.
> I send a letter, other hands will tear it
> Before its words can ever reach her eyes:
> I send my love to her: yet I do fear it
> That if she ever knows of it, she dies
> > In that close prison where she lies
> > Confined alone
> > In cruel walls of stone
> By one she loved yet now must needs despise.

FITZWALTER. Confined alone by whom?

YOUNG MARSHAL. Her husband.

DE VESCI. Did John send you here to sing that?

YOUNG MARSHAL. Certainly not. It has nothing whatever to do with John. It was written to his mother when Henry Curtmantle had her in gaol for conspiracy. An old lover of hers – a poet from Carcassonne –

DE VESCI (*leaping up suddenly*). They call it the Morpeth Rant: It's a grand stamping dance, I've seen my boors do it in Northumbria – it goes best with the big boots on – the sheep-herders dance it on the hill – there's none of your Provençal adulteries about *this* –

He starts singing, clapping his hands on the beat, then launches

E

into a dance. The others (except YOUNG MARSHAL), *join in one by one. The tune is a reel, but they do not dance it that way – they merely prance round in a circle one after the other, making a great deal of noise.*

Oh *what* will you gie me if I knock you in the teeth, boy,
What will you gie me if I kick your *gut?*
A *knife* in the belly and a club upon the headpiece,
That's what ye're wanting, it's what you'll *get!*

Oh nights are dark and days are cold
And life is short and the world is long
And left is right and right is wrong
And who put the wolf in the *old* sheep fold?

There's only the one set of words, we sing them round and round until we're sick of it –
> *He tries to pull the Lady into the dance, but she evades him and goes out.*
> *As she goes out, she drops her kerchief.* YOUNG MARSHAL *picks it up, but when he offers it her, she makes a gesture refusing it. He puts it quickly in his breast.*

– *She's* sick of it already, and not before time – come on –
> *The dance continues, until interrupted by voices off.*

1ST VOICE (*off*). No you may not go up, the Barons are in private –

2ND VOICE (*off*). They are taking their pleasure, sir, you are not to disturb them –
> *The* MAYOR *bursts in, despite efforts of some* SERVANTS *to restrain him.*

MAYOR. No man tells the Mayor of London 'not' within the walls of his own city. My Lords, London has her liberties, established, enrolled, and sealed. I am delegate by free choice of our citizens to affirm and to guard the enfranchise of this town.

FITZWALTER. I think you forget yourself, sir.

MAYOR. It may be so, my Lord. It may indeed be very possibly so. The words which I have had occasion to make use of, I made use of, let me in all honesty inform you, as the words of a Gown and Chain, not as the words of a common citizen. The Gown and Chain being susceptible to the corruption (as I believe it is spoken in Scripture) of moth and rust alone: and moth and rust, with due care – that is to say, polishing, oiling, dusting, and the application of camphor – we may very easily inhibit. But as to the corruptions to which the mortal human frame is susceptible, and not only the frame, but the spirit within it, these with naught but grave difficulty are to be avoided. Are they not, young women?

He looks keenly at the BLONDE GIRL.

I knew your father. I knew him for a good man. Poor, but honest, though indeed no more than a fishporter – goes to Mass and pays his dues most regularly. Will I tell him you are here?

BLONDE GIRL. Perhaps he sent me.

MAYOR. No, he did not send you.

DARK GIRL. Didn't he? Trade's poor at the fishmarket.

MAYOR. But there are other markets, are there not? I mean, for the stinking fish – you take my meaning, don't you? And with a town full of soldiers as this town is at present – (*He looks at the* DARK GIRL.) You were whipped two months ago, I recollect it well, at *my* orders from the Bench, for pursuit of that same unchaste market – (*To the* RED HAIRED GIRL.) and I fancy you were too, young lady, weren't you? Or if you weren't you should have been.

DE VESCI. Tell him go and take his market to the bottom of the river – fish market, haddock, cod's head, red herring . . .

FITZWALTER. That will do, Eustace. We are the Mayor of London's guests in London, don't forget: but these little nightingales are *our* guests and we are under no obligation to have them questioned here.

MAYOR. That may be as it may be, my Lord, indeed, very

much it may be, yes. But I had in mind this evening, upon coming here to speak with you, to put down before you, my Lord, in straight cuts with no frayed edges –

YOUNG MARSHAL. Frayed edges – I don't quite –

DE VESCI. The man's a draper – he sells cloth – frayed edges unravel. Well, stop unravelling: talk!

MAYOR. Very good, my Lord: as you put it. There is an established paragraph in the Charter, granting the complete liberties of the City of London. Without frayed edges, my Lord, that paragraph was put in for the purpose of a fair contract. You want a basis to establish your force. We are commercial men here and we enter contract with you to grant you a lease of the walls of this city, and the price is our liberty. Very well, then: tit-for-tat.

FITZWALTER. Tit-for-tat-what?

MAYOR (*indicates* GIRLS). Now take these for a start. It is well understood, and though we may not all confess to such habits, being, as you will very well say, by nature of our trade, as a draper or a goldsmith or a shoemaker or such-like, necessarily sober men and decorously-conducted, and notwithstanding noblemen upon military emergency are commonly granted the sort of pleasures befitting their rank, and certainly not myself nor anyone else would speak a word against it. But the town is full of soldiers, out of all rank and station, and they're all up to the same game, and we'd be better off with the French here, or even the King's Flemings! How long it's going to last, I don't know and nobody does, but the behaviour of your troops is an offence in our nostrils and it was not to cause this that the Charter was drawn up! No, my Lord, no – I speak by Gown and Chain!

DE VESCI. You speak by profit and loss.

FITZWALTER. For you have made commercial contract not only with ourselves but also with the King. Did he not grant to the city of London its own Mayoral Charter not one month before he met us at Runnymede, and was not the

purpose of that Mayoral Charter to secure the city to him in
the event of civil war, and did not we offer you a higher
price in our Charter and beat him at his bargain? You choose
to condemn these daughters of your liberty, but what have
they done that you have not, Master Mayor?

YOUNG MARSHAL. Do we wish to make a quarrel here with
this good man, or what? Sir, I will offer you a cup of wine.
Be so good as to drink it. What you speak, you speak
seriously – though inhibited perhaps by our superior rank –
and therefore you should be listened to. Will you please
drink?   ..

MAYOR. I will with pleasure accept your refreshment. I thank
you, my Lord . . . Grave concern; doubts and hesitations, not
only for myself but the Aldermen, the Masters of the City
Companies, the entire mercantile body – we are gravely
concerned and indeed have taken counsel together. It is not
only the matter of the turbulent soldiery for which in regard
to my recent outburst of anger I crave pardon – but a serious
and deep consideration for our essential purposes at this
time. The King has promised to govern his realm with what
amounts to justice and restraint. He has taken note –

FITZWALTER. He has been forced to take note.

MAYOR. – of the demands of the nobility, and the church, and
also the commercial interests for the first time in history.
Forced, yes, my Lord, and forced by your soldiers – that is,
the nobility alone. The church, when she was alone in the
time of the Interdict, failed to coerce him: and we, as men of
commerce, are of course men of peace – we have but our
wharves and counting-houses and our profit and loss.
Therefore we depend on you: and we depend on your
honour. We have let you into London for your manifest
advantage: *our* manifest advantage, my Lord, is a complete
and equitable enforcement of the entire Charter, no clause
of it bated, and with no distortion of its purposes. Are you
prepared to grant us that?

FITZWALTER. I was under the impression that you and the
Army of God were in a free alliance together to bring down
King John. You are remarkably solicitous of the con-
venience of your enemy, sir. Of course – I had forgotten, he
helped you build your bridge.

MAYOR. A bridge is important to us, my Lord, we are a great
city with great traffic. Besides, there is a rhyme already
current in the ale-houses concerning that same bridge.

To RED HAIRED GIRL *who has laughed.*

I expect *you* know it, don't you?

RED HAIRED GIRL.

As I was going o'er London Bridge
I heard something crack.
Not a man in all England
Can mend a crack like that.

The GIRLS *laugh.*

MAYOR. It is only a probable prophecy – as yet. Do we want it
to be true? (*He looks at his wine.*) A very reputable friend of
mine imports this, from Gascony. The last shipload to come
in, he had had to dodge for three days through the Channel
Islands to get it past the pirates. For them it would have
been a diversion to catch a cargo of good wine: for him and
for his sailormen, my Lords, their life and death – no less!
But the point that I would make by the mention of it now is
that I would not have you think that I would speak against
diversions. I was invited to a tournament – an agreeable
diversion, both for me and my family, pageantry of arms,
yes, a very gallant spectacle . . . But suppose now that your
tournament, upon duly commencing, were never to con-
clude? That we'd to sit still out at Hounslow for all the rest
of the year, all the rest of our lives, and with nothing to do
but watch horses and riders in a big field at Hounslow knock
each other over? I mean it'd be ridiculous – wouldn't it?
We'd get no business done. And what's more to the purpose
is that none of the competitors would ever win a prize. Now

then: no frayed edges – when are your soldiers going to be removed?

DE VESCI. We never remove soldiers. Not one drunken defaulter. Never remove soldiers.

YOUNG MARSHAL. But I told you – my father's chaplain told me that the King has written letters –

DE VESCI. Oh those letters, that . . . flatfish, mudfish, hake –

MAYOR. My Lord, what letters? Letters to whom?

YOUNG MARSHAL. There are to be no more mercenaries come to the King from Flanders. It is a solemn undertaking. There is absolutely no reason why we should not disband.

MAYOR. Indeed no, there is not – at least if the report is true.

YOUNG MARSHAL. My father has pledged his word that it is.

MAYOR. Then, my Lord, it must be. Why did you not think fit to inform me about these letters, gentlemen? I am asking for an answer.

There is a pause. The GIRLS *are getting restive.*

DARK GIRL. If we're not wanted here, we can always go away.

BLONDE GIRL. We're not short of business, you know, not with all the soldiers in town.

DE VESCI (*rounding upon her*). What did you say!

BLONDE GIRL. Nothing, milord, really, I beg pardon, milord.

YOUNG MARSHAL (*to* GIRLS). Go on, the three of you – out. The porter at the door will give you your money – go on.

The GIRLS *go out.*

MAYOR. I am asking for an answer, and I am still waiting, my Lord.

FITZWALTER. The Feast of the Assumption.

MAYOR. I beg your pardon, my Lord?

FITZWALTER. I do not intend to modify the dispositions of the Army of God until the Feast of the Assumption. It has been agreed at Oxford. You must be satisfied with that.

MAYOR. I cannot pretend I am: and I cannot pretend that the people of London are going to be, either.

FITZWALTER. The ladies who have just left us may not share your opinion.

MAYOR. Conceivably not. However, I will wait upon events. The Feast of the Assumption is not very far away. Good night to you, my Lords.

YOUNG MARSHAL. I will accompany you, sir. I am sure that we can do something to improve the discipline of our troops. I would be glad to discuss it with you. Good night, Eustace. Good night, Robert.

Exeunt MAYOR *and* YOUNG MARSHAL.

DE VESCI (*looking at where the* GIRLS *have sat*). Where did they go to?

FITZWALTER. Who?

DE VESCI. Ah, never mind. They were but a moment's distraction, the old malignant mortification remains. Whether he hires his lances from Flanders or not, whether there is a war or whether there is not: it would be nothing less than lunacy to disband at this moment.

FITZWALTER. I agree. John has always ruled this kingdom as though it were his own private farmyard and we were his pigs, and he is not going to change his habits now, because of words upon a parchment. We can wait until the Assumption.

DE VESCI. And then we can wait until –

FITZWALTER. The next feast-day, or the next. In the meantime my messengers are at the court of the King of France. If we need his help he'll give it, but I hope he won't have to.

DE VESCI. Indeed by God's Bones I hope he won't have to. There is one King too many in this country already.

FITZWALTER. France should be well accustomed to being controlled by his great barons. I anticipate no problem there.

DE VESCI. Where did they go to?

FITZWALTER. Young Marshal sent them fluttering.

DE VESCI. He takes too much upon himself. He is too young to take so much. He is the son of his father. (*He looks vaguely round, as if for his wife.*) And where has the other one gone? By God, she is an ulcer developing under the plaster of wedlock . . . How far will you let John gallop you before you send for the King of France?

FITZWALTER. The moment it is clear to everyone, including young Marshal, including his archaic father, including the Archbishop –

DE VESCI. And also the Mayor of London –

FITZWALTER. And also the Mayor of London, that King Softsword as much desires as we do to carve up this useless Charter – straight cuts and no frayed edges – that moment we send word to France. Are you with me?

DE VESCI. Without question. God's Nostrils, where's she got to? She was in here but one minute since . . .

He moves drunkenly out.

FITZWALTER *laughs, finishes his wine, and goes out at the opposite door.*

SCENE THREE

Enter PANDULPH.

PANDULPH. Confronted as we are by the apparent spectacle of depravity, treachery and violent self-seeking upon both sides of this miserable dispute, let us not too readily dismiss that aspect of human nature, which, in even the worst of men, contains some yearning for the paths of virtue. Hypocrisy, as exemplified in a Fitzwalter or a de Vesci, nevertheless pays tribute to idealism insofar as it finds it necessary to cloak its evil purposes under the disguise of a worthy cause. The cause, in this instance, I have already shewn to be futile – but never mind: it exists.

As for King John himself – that almost Oriental monster of your history books – do not forget that the records of his Household shew him to have been a tireless administrator, devoted to the pursuit of justice – albeit wrongheadedly, as many would maintain. Day by day, even in the midst of profound political turbulence, he traversed his realm, continually in the saddle, continually hearing causes, receiving petitions, inquiring into abuses . . .

He sits down in his chair.

SCENE FOUR

A picture of an apple orchard, formally drawn, with large fruit on the branches, flowers in the grass, and many birds and little animals.

Enter JOHN, *from riding, together with his travelling-party – the* QUEEN, PRINCE HENRY, LADY DE VESCI, MARSHAL, CLERKS *and other attendants.*

A camp stool is brought for the King, the rest sit down around him on the grass, while a picnic meal is served by the Attendants. Throughout the scene, this meal is being eaten – JOHN *in particular eats a very great deal.*

JOHN. We have travelled far enough this morning – let them serve us with a little food and drink. Here, serve it here . . . I have always been of the opinion that the Southern Counties of England contain the fairest prospects of nature to be found throughout my territory. Observe this agreeable Kentish orchard, where the golden apples on the autumn trees hang waiting for the husbandmen to gather them in to their baskets. An appropriate place, my lords and ladies, for a king in an old legend to sit and dispense justice to his subjects, untroubled by factious discord. Remember what was said of the brave and scholarly King Alfred – that at the end of his reign it was possible for a man to hang golden drinking cups beside a simple wayside fountain, and to have no fear that they would be stolen – or even borrowed. If I in my due time could be laid in a tomb with that epitaph graven over it, I could then regard myself as a fit successor to my famous father. As for my no less famous mother, her beautiful, stubborn, and deceitful spirit has so wound itself into my uncomely body, that not only does my right hand not know what my left hand is doing, – which is indeed recommended in the Holy Gospel – but actual bloody conflict between these two unhappy members prevails every day of my life. Look, the cruel nails of the one dig into the flesh of the other until the white skin is marked with scarlet – a man might believe I was an impoverished smallholder struggling eternally to clear brambles from my land. And even in my domestic affairs old Eleanor still infects me. Here I sit, a Queen on the one side, a mistress on the other . . . or *is* she? At any rate her husband thinks so. And she has happily found ways to escape from his loathsome bed.

LADY DE VESCI. Arduous and surreptitious ways – corruption of servants, melodramatic performances with ropes of knotted sheets hung out of windows, riding on a wild night cloaked and hooded like a highwayman – and not even efficient. I suppose I should at least have brought you some sketch plans of the fortifications of London.

JOHN. God will provide the sketch plans. Saucy Castle fell and Saucy Castle was held by men of great integrity. But you have provided me, my lady, with intelligence of far higher value – a keen description and diagnosis of what is going on inside the muddy mind of my enemies . . . other ladies also have – provided me, in their time. I have no less than five bastards scattered about my dominions, and five legitimate children likewise – (*He puts his arm round* PRINCE HENRY.) – of whom this one here is to become the King of England. You do realise that, my pretty careless boy? It may happen to you quite soon . . . And yet no-one can say that my marital infidelities have detracted any whit from the love I bear my wife.

QUEEN.
When I was but twelve years old

I was betrothed to a lord of France:
But the wild King of England grinned over the garden wall
Where I and my little maidens did dance.

JOHN.

She was as beautiful and delicate a child
As ever I had seen.
And upon that sunlit afternoon
I determined she would be my queen.

QUEEN.

For four years I grew
Through my short ungainly puberty
And at the end of that time
When he knew my woman's beauty
I held him in such thrall
That he lost the whole of Normandy.

JOHN.

It has been alleged
In terms of political scandal
That we took so long time in our tent
On a morning to kiss and fondle
That the battle was lost and broken
And Saucy Castle taken
And yet no man could stir me to rise.
It was more than a scandal
It was in fact a pack of lies.
Yet my mother would say:
If I did not find this story flattering,
By so much the less
Was I truly a king.

*There is some whispering and shifting about among the
Attendants – the* CLERK *comes to the King.*

CLERK. My Lord, there are two parties here to a lawsuit – the
plaintiff is anxious that you yourself should give him a
judgement.

JOHN. Certainly not. I am eating my dinner. Have we no

Circuit Courts in the County of Kent? Have we no Justices? Why should they trouble *me* – they invariably trouble *me* – they do not seem to realize that the King cannot personally be expected to handle – and yet, do I not remember saying during the negotiations over the Charter that I never deny right and justice? How long will they have to wait if they wait for the regular Judge?

CLERK. They have been waiting for five years, my Lord – the administrative delays have been –

JOHN. Five years? Intolerable! Inquire into it at once, and see that somebody is punished. Heavily. Punish them with a fine. Always a fine, remember: we have rebellions on hand, we are always in need of money. Very well, the litigants may appear before us, bring them along.

The GOLDSMITH, *his* WIFE *and the* PARSON *are brought in.*

Now then, good people, don't be afraid. I am the King, but I rule under Providence of God, and a small portion at least of His Divine Mercy is ever present in my spirit. Tell me your names and station.

GOLDSMITH. My name is Cuthbert of Dover, sire. I am a goldsmith.

JOHN. In a poor way of business, to judge from your appearance. Are you no good at your trade?

GOLDSMITH. I lay claim to be a master of my trade, my Lord. The pendant that this woman wears is of my own workmanship.

JOHN. Let's have a look at it . . . I know something about jewels . . . A true lovers' knot in gold wire enclosing five garnet stones – why, it is very beautiful, Cuthbert: and so are the breasts upon which it is depending. To whom do they belong?

GOLDSMITH. She is my wife, my Lord.

JOHN. I was asking her, not you. What is your name, sweetheart? Tell it, to your King.

GOLDSMITH'S WIFE. Jennifer, my Lord.

JOHN. Jennifer – what kind of a name is that?

LADY DE VESCI. It is a rustic corruption of Guinevere – King Arthur's adulterous queen.

JOHN. Oh. I hope it isn't catching. And the reverend gentleman over there – who are you?

PARSON. I am the Parish Priest of St Mary in Dover, my Lord: my name is Thomas.

JOHN. Very well. Who's the plaintiff? . . . Cuthbert? Set forward your plea.

GOLDSMITH. This so-called celibate priest, my Lord, five years ago, seduced the affections of my wife and she has cohabited with him in his parsonage ever since. With me she had no children: she has borne him a daughter.

JOHN. Has she indeed? How old are you?

GOLDSMITH. Forty-eight, my Lord.

JOHN. So am I. A middle-aged man with a young wife ought to know how to treat her well enough to prevent her being carried away by the Parson. But precisely what are you asking me for?

GOLDSMITH. Damages, my Lord. I have been made a mock and a scorn among the people of Dover, and my business has greatly suffered as a result. The rude boys in the street replaced my shop-sign only last year with a pair of cow's horns and an upturned chalice. This sort of nonsense has been going on all the time. I shall be ruined if I get no satisfaction.

JOHN. Sir Thomas, come here . . . stout, red-faced, pleasant-looking, young . . . Yes, I can understand it. But this is really an ecclesiastical matter, surely, your Bishop ought to – oh God no, we're in Canterbury's Diocese here, that prelate is concerned with far different business! Lady, what is your opinion?

QUEEN. I think he is entitled to damages. The priest is too handsome. He should never have allowed a body like that to be sequestered by the Church; he must pay some compensation to the World for depriving us of its merits.

JOHN (*to* LADY DE VESCI). And your opinion, madam?

LADY DE VESCI. The child. Is she malformed?

JOHN. Well, is she?

GOLDSMITH'S WIFE. Oh no milord, milady – er milord – no . . .

LADY DE VESCI. Is she beautiful?

GOLDSMITH'S WIFE. *I* think so, yes.

LADY DE VESCI. Then there can be no disgrace in her creation. It is not a fit subject for mockery.

JOHN. Even if she were malformed, it would not be a fit subject for mockery. (*To* GOLDSMITH.) You were unable to provide a child for this woman: the priest has obligingly fulfilled your function for you. How did he succeed in seducing you, Jennifer?

GOLDSMITH'S WIFE. Milord, he plays the mandoline – he sang me ballads in the vestry.

JOHN. Excellent, by God, yes! Have you anything to say, Sir Thomas? Can you deny the accusation? . . . Then you had better not speak at all. Your mandoline has already said far too much. You will pay this good man fifty shillings for the loss of his wife and his reputation, and fifty shillings to me, as a fine for your misconduct. If this were heard in the Archbishop's Court, they'd extort a good deal more, so I warn you not to stand upon the privilege of your cloth. Cuthbert Goldsmith, you likewise will pay me fifty shillings as a fee for my hearing the case and for the interruption of my picnic. That will perhaps teach you to be more tender to young women. Wives are not chattels. I can see by the hang of your nostril that you thought that yours was. However, as the pendant that she is wearing really is extremely beautiful, I shall take order that you be appointed a Craftsman to the Royal Household, and that you shall have the charge of the maintenance of our own jewellery when we are in the Southern Parts. Open that box, Augustine, and take out the little cap badge with the sapphires in it.

    The CLERK *finds the badge in a jewel box which the King has had by him.*

One of the stones is working loose from the setting. Will you please repair it for me directly?

GOLDSMITH (*taking the jewel*). With pleasure, my Lord, with great pleasure, indeed it is an honour . . .

JOHN. Off you go now. Augustine, go with them and see that the money is properly transferred . . . Oh, one moment – the woman stays with the priest. Now we are no longer under an Interdict, it is none of my business to interfere with the private lives of clerics. But take heed the Archdeacon doesn't catch you at your games. Good-bye.

    Exeunt LITIGANTS, *with* CLERK.

And good riddance . . . What's the matter, William, you are looking upon me with a lack-lustre eye?

MARSHAL. From my limited experience of the Law, sire, I would have thought that your handling of this case was not quite in accordance with precedent.

JOHN. Oh yes, I daresay – but was it not just? In fact, a new precedent has now been established: and all judges in the future – I hope – may understand therefrom that there is no substitute for direct comprehension and even enjoyment of the individual humours of each person brought before them. I have left all three of them satisfied. What more could they want?

    YOUNG MARSHAL *enters rapidly, with a drawn sword. He is wearing* LADY DE VESCI's *kerchief in his helmet.*

And Judas' Neckbone – what do *you* want? It was in our mind, young sir, that you were confederate with the body of our enemies at present holding garrison in the City of London! Marshal, put your insensate child under arrest.

YOUNG MARSHAL. I came here with a mounted escort. Do you want a battle? I am ready to oblige – I notice your own escort is considerably smaller – though it might disarrange the ladies.

LADY DE VESCI. That is a noble sentiment, sir. I notice from the favour in your helmet that you are a gentleman of true chivalrous practice – though surely you did not come here solely to proclaim the virtues of your beloved?

YOUNG MARSHAL. No: I did not. I wish that I had. It is a different aspect of knightly honour that has compelled me here today.

MARSHAL. Do you dare to speak of honour in the same voice with which you threaten battle to your King, sir! You shall indeed have your battle – there are more loyal soldiers in this county than you can see at this moment, and I am the commander of them!

YOUNG MARSHAL. Of all of them, father? Including the ones who are to arrive in Dover harbour as soon as the winds are favourable? I fancy they will bring their own general with them – Sir Hugh de Boves, from Flanders.

MARSHAL. What!

YOUNG MARSHAL. The Papal Legate is not the only man who can dispose of an intelligence service across the Channel. We have discovered that a large army of mercenaries is assembled at Antwerp and will sail before Michaelmas. Why else do you think the King's Progress keeps so tightly to the Kentish Coast?

MARSHAL. This must be one of Fitzwalter's lies. It must. Sire, I appeal to you at once to deny this vicious calumny.

JOHN. No. No, I can't deny it, Marshal; it happens to be true. Now, this is going to put your loyalty to quite an extensive test, is it not? But I will demonstrate my justification. This angry Paladin, here, your son, originally joined with Fitzwalter's party because he was of the honest opinion that the Customs of England needed to be codified and clarified under due process of law. I believe in his honesty – he has inherited many virtues from you. And yet, after only a year

F

from his first association with that riotous gang, he storms in upon his King and presents him with the blade of a falchion! Thus you will observe the treason and corruption that still maintains its lair within the walls of London Town. If I bring in no army, I shall be naked in their hands.

MARSHAL. But, sire, the words of the Charter – what about the Charter, sire?

PANDULPH (*coming forward with a letter*). I think I had best explain to everyone the present state of the Charter. I have received a letter from His Holiness Pope Innocent. He writes:

'We have heard that the King of England has been forced to accept an agreement which is not only shameful and base, but also illegal and unjust. We refuse to pass over such shameful presumption; for the Apostolic See would be dishonoured, the King's right injured, the English nation shamed, and the whole plan for the Crusade seriously endangered. Therefore we utterly reject and condemn this settlement and under threat of excommunication we order that the King should not dare to observe it and the Barons and their associates should not insist on its being observed. The Charter itself we declare to be null and void of all validity, for ever.'

JOHN. It would indeed be a pity to endanger my plan for the Crusade.

He pulls the copy of the Charter down and tears it up.

YOUNG MARSHAL. The son of the French King once before laid claim to the Throne of England. If he chooses to renew that claim, in person, at the head of an army, I do not see how the barons in London are to be prevented from supporting him. The liberties of the English people will not be increased by such a procedure.

Exeunt.

Act Three

A large map of England replaces the Charter opposite Pandulph's chair.

    An icon-like illustration of the murder of Becket.

    Enter ARCHBISHOP.

ARCHBISHOP.

    Once in the land of Babylon,
    Which was then called Babel,
    Ingenious and inventive men
    Believed themselves able
    To erect the greatest tower
    That ever had been built.
    Architect, mason, carpenter, plumber –
    Craftsmen in brick, stone, lead and timber –
    For all one year they worked:
    And all their work was spilt.
    As you will very well remember
    It was the Hand of God
    That struck them to confusion,
    Planting upon their tongues
    The discord of His derision,
    Making every man's design
    Incomprehensible to his neighbour.
    No tower was completed,
    No wages were paid for all that long labour,
    For all that pride there were no rewards,
    Nothing but a maze of bewildering words –
    And that was far worse than nothing at all.

      PANDULPH *has quietly taken his seat.*

PANDULPH. If you mean to imply, Your Grace, that this

unexpected letter from the Pope is the result of the pride of those overweening barons who corrupted your own good intentions, I will not contradict you. But I would also point out that His Holiness has included you, specifically, in his indictment. He writes, in a second letter –

See how Stephen of Canterbury and his fellow-bishops defy the patrimony of the Roman Church! See how they protect Crusaders!

Indeed, he goes on to say that you are worse than the Saracens, because the Saracens at least are the declared enemies of Christ, while the Bishops of England – I will not grieve your heart further. What do you intend to do?

ARCHBISHOP. If I do not submit to the Pope and obey him, I presume you are empowered to suspend me from my Archbishopric?

PANDULPH. Yes.

ARCHBISHOP. Thomas Becket, when driven out of England by the King, lived for several years the life of a humble brother in a French cloister. I have considered doing the same myself. I have even considered preparing a formal statement of penitence for ever having allowed myself to meddle with the temporal affairs and advocate the liberties of the people of England. But such a self-surrender has never been truly Stephen. I have believed always in the strength of the sword in the hand of Jesus – I mean the sword that will cleave directly through to the betterment of mankind. I do not mean the sword of war – the text is misread if you think so, and you do think so, there are many here that do think so, Simon Peter used that stupid sword in the garden to cut off the ear of a catchpole who was doing no more than earning his daily pay. But we know what happened to the ear that was cut off and we read no more words in the Gospel of the sword that did cut it. No, Pandulph: I will neither submit, nor obey, nor resign. I will carry my sword to Rome and explain to the Pope, who was once my very dear friend, precisely what was meant by the Charter which the King sealed. For my Charter – no, not *my* Charter, the Charter of the English – it is not the Tower of Babel – it will not lie for ever a heap of rain-washed ruin for the donkeys to stale upon and the serpents to breed in the holes of its brickwork – and the Pope must know that it will not.

PANDULPH. But what is the Charter, after all? An up-to-date version of some promises once made by King Henry I? Even taken at best, it has no eternal validity. What is it, what is it?

ARCHBISHOP. Even taken at worst, it is a statement, well-intentioned and futile, if you like – but a precise statement, Pandulph. I thought, in the beginning, it was perhaps no more than a convenient device to hold off for a while the fury of the barons. The King took it as such, and was grateful, he made remarkably little objection to it, under the circumstances. But when I was compelled to admit to myself that (as soon as it had served its original purpose) neither the barons nor the King were likely to take note of it, then I began to realise that the words that it contained, having been said once and having been written down, could no more be blotted out by King, Baron or Pope even, than I can deny the Divinity of My Saviour.

PANDULPH. Aha, I did suspect it. You attribute your own fallible words to the breath of the Holy Spirit. I hope you understand that you are practically in heresy.

ARCHBISHOP. It is nothing whatever to do with heresy, Pandulph. Will you please not endeavour to intimidate me, sir! I am speaking of a document that is the necessary fulfill-ment of the existing Laws and Customs of this land. Such has not been made before, but we have made it now. The Kings and Lords of England, who will in the future need authority, who will need a definite statement of what they may not do and what may not be done to them – these men will look to it and I believe that they will thank us for it. But not unless the Charter is able to survive. To ensure its survival, I must plead with the Pope. I would not care to accuse the Holy Father of ignorance, but there are nevertheless a few matters concerning England upon which, I suspect, he has been deliberately misinformed.

Exit ARCHBISHOP.

SCENE TWO

Pictures of warfare – men-at-arms fighting, houses burning, refugees, etc.

PANDULPH. Which words – like an ill-directed arrow – do not strike at my heart. Because Pope Innocent III has the most beautiful intellect of any man ever to have occupied the Chair of St Peter: and if he should choose to see England and the affairs of England in a correct proportion relative to the affairs of the entire world, I do not propose to run counter to his opinion. I am a native of Pisa. Archbishop Stephen – the erstwhile Archbishop Stephen – was (I believe) born in the County of Lincoln. There is a difference.

A very short recital of the warfare which followed the papal repudiation of the Charter. I know little about such matters, but I am informed by those who are more expert, that had King John struck directly at London before the barons could receive their reinforcement from France, he might well have succeeded in crushing the rebellion at once. However, he did not.

The first detachment of Flemings to cross the Channel to the King was wrecked in a great storm: the rebels took advantage and occupied Rochester. The King laid siege to Rochester and it surrendered – November 30th, 1215. The greater part of the barons' army – large but ill-organized – remained in London, where they were joined about this time by an inconsiderable body of French. There were

pockets of baronial adherents in different parts of the
country – particularly the east and north, but disconnected
and vulnerable.

He is pointing all this out on the map.

John, balking, as I say, at a decisive attack upon London,
determined instead to eliminate the pockets. 'Elimination of
pockets' is a craftsmanlike term much employed by those
cruel and skilful men who hire out their services from
Flanders. It means, of course, the complete destruction of
castles, houses, barns, livestock, fishing-boats, windmills,
watermills, granaries, the bodies of men, the chastity of
women – I speak nothing of children. I would merely
remind you that this happened in the months of December
and January, and it happened from here –

St Albans on the map.

to *here* –

Berwick-upon-Tweed, on the map.

and back again, in February, *here.*

Suffolk and Essex, on the map.

This happened, in winter, in England, under the orders of a
King of England, and at the hands of a foreign army. Many
of you, no doubt, will think that I do wrong to lay the
responsibility for such wickedness upon the profound and
good intentions of Archbishop Stephen Langton. And yet,
I do so lay it. His duty to his Church was clear and he denied
it. He believed he had been working, in a kind of parenthesis,
not for the Church of Christ, but for the amelioration of
England – and you have heard the result.

No such belief has attended the deliberations of the King of
France. His desire, quite simply, has been to enlarge his
boundaries, and to do so, if possible, in an odour of sanctity.
I take pains to point out that this will not be possible.

The month of April, 1216: France.

SCENE THREE

The Lilies of France.

Enter PHILIP, LOUIS, BLANCHE.

PANDULPH (*to audience still*). King Philip Augustus; Louis, his
eldest son; Blanche, the wife of Louis. The boundaries of
King Philip have been in process of enlargement for many
years: and for the most part at the expense of England. He
has already, in 1212, considered placing an army across the
Channel –

   He now speaks to Philip.

But in that year, my Lord, King John was excommunicated.
Had you put to sea then, you might have flown the Papal
Ensign at your masthead and sailed as upon Crusade. Today
however, the barbed hook of St Peter sticks in the throat of a
different fish.

PHILIP. These reversals of fortune, Master Legate, are the lot
of mankind. It would not be seemly to rail against them. But
nobility and royalty are not to be put down by such temporary accidents. France is a Catholic Kingdom, and we
trust that whether or no the Pope should smile upon our
enterprise, God will always continue to do so. He has indeed
put into my mind a means of overcoming this present small
obstacle. My learned men have elaborated a formula. Listen.
King John claims that he handed his crown to the Pope and
received it back upon terms of feudal service. But he cannot
have done this –

LOUIS. Because it was not his to give.

PANDULPH. Indeed, my Lord? Whose was it?

LOUIS. We'll come to that in a moment. When Richard
Lionheart was alive and imprisoned by the Duke of Austria,
John laid plots against him –

PHILIP. And consequently, in King Richard's own Court, was
adjudged a proven traitor.

LOUIS. That judgement has never been rescinded. Therefore
when King Richard Lionheart died –

PHILIP. It was incorrect and illegal for the Lords of England
to place John upon his throne. They should have chosen –

LOUIS. Arthur, who was the son of the elder brother of John,
and who, alas, unfortunate child that he was –

PHILIP. Was brutally murdered, by John.

LOUIS. France, you will remember, espoused the cause of
Arthur at that time. And therefore, Arthur being dead, and
the Crown of England usurped, the true heir to England's
throne must be sought and found –

PHILIP. Among the surviving progeny of the other brothers
and sisters of John. Of whom the most eligible turns out to
be the Lady Blanche: here she is, grand-daughter to King
Henry Curtmantle of England, and married –

LOUIS. To me.

PANDULPH. Oh happy lady, happy prince, happy King. A
jocund family of dynastic lawyers indeed. Would that I
could immerse myself, my lords, in chopping your logic with
you: there is nothing I enjoy better. But no, I fear not: my
instructions are precise. Curt, in fact, to the point of
vulgarity. If France invades the realm of England, France
will be excommunicate and that is all there is to it.

PHILIP. Master Legate, France is Catholic, and dutiful.
Therefore, Prince Louis, as your liege lord and as your
Catholic father, we forbid you in the sternest words to offer
aid or succour to the irreligious barons of England.

LOUIS (*kneeling*). Sire, as your Catholic vassal and your most
submissive son, I humbly accept your necessary orders. But
Blanche my wife has a rightful claim to be the Queen of
England. You have no power to withhold her from that
claim. Neither have you power to withhold me from helping
her. (*He gets up again.*) She is but a weak woman and she
needs her husband's sword.

BLANCHE (*to* PHILIP). Brother of France, when we achieve

in fact that crown which is already ours in right and title,
there shall be no bounds put to the gratitude and friendship
which you may demand of us.

PHILIP. We accept with appropriate grace your graceful
sentiment, madam: and may the Hand of God confirm your
just prosperity.

PANDULPH. The Hand of God has been invoked by a great
many people lately. I wonder are we not perhaps in danger
of confounding our Divine Redeemer with those obscene
idols of the Orient that Crusaders talk of – I mean the ones
with six or seven arms growing out of a single body?

Exeunt PHILIP, LOUIS and BLANCHE.

They do not care to listen to my homilies, which is under-
standable. They are altogether too intelligent not to be
aware of what they are doing. God has but two hands. To
attempt to dispose of their benefits upon earth without due
authority is to court damnation –

SCENE FOUR

*A picture of armed soldiers standing in close ranks, with banners
etc., and the tops of tents behind them.*

Enter JOHN.

PANDULPH. They are courting damnation, my Lord.

JOHN. They are also courting defeat. I have a navy. The
coast of England is impregnable.

Enter MARSHAL *and* OFFICERS.

MARSHAL. No, my Lord. God, with the adverse winds at His
command, and no doubt for some inscrutable purpose of His
own, has scattered your navy; and the French fleet has safely
passed the mouth of Pegwell Bay. Prince Louis has established his camp upon the northern coast of Kent, and those
rebels whom you thought you had subdued in the winter
have once more plucked up their courage. The King of

Scotland has led an army of his own across the Border against you, and far too many of your mercenary soldiers have not received their pay. What is to be done?

JOHN. Not received their pay . . . what is to be done . . . They will get their pay, God's Bread, sir, when they have fulfilled their contract! Let them drive the Frenchmen out. Until they have done that for me, how can I scrabble for money? I have gone into this before – how many times I don't know – that I do not understand, and nobody understands, where the money comes from or where it goes to when it has been spent. If some new Aristotle could develop a science out of that, perhaps we could then know how to govern our people. Had Stephen Langton studied in Paris the pilgrimage of money instead of the pilgrimage of the soul, he might never have needed to frame that destructive Charter, which thank God has ruined him as bitterly as it is ruining me – and yet again, he might . . . Nearly twelve hundred years since Christ gave the Word, and theology knows no more than ever it did – so why should we expect better from any experts in finance? Perhaps some extraordinary taxation, fines for delinquencies, forced loans from the Jews – look into it, Marshal, are they possible, are they?

FIRST OFFICER. Why, your entire kingdom is one black gangrene of warfare – of course they are not possible.

MARSHAL. So what is to be done?

JOHN. Which garrisons are threatened? I mean, which important ones?

SECOND OFFICER (*at map*). Louis controls Kent, Surrey, and Sussex. The Army of God –

MARSHAL. – the excommunicate Army of God –

SECOND OFFICER. – is besieging Windsor and Dover. As before, their principal camp is London. The Scots are besieging Barnard Castle, here, and Durham, here. We still have freedom of manoeuvre in the midlands and south-west.

JOHN. London. The chief city of my realm and the chief city

of my enemies. They have been in London now for over a
year. And yet not only their army but the citizens are
excommunicated. I know Fitzwalter and de Vesci would not
give the snot from their nostrils for the consolations of Holy
Church, but I should have thought that to the merchants, to
the craft-guilds, to the street-singers and the parish clergy,
to the watermen on the Thames – and particularly to their
wives, such matters of eternity would be of some importance. They made enough hurly-burly, did they not, when
the Interdict was laid upon ourself? And why are they not
terrified, when they regard the results of my progress to the
north last winter? Let them consider what I did to the Palati-
nate of Durham and to Berwick-upon-Tweed. Do they want
Cheapside and Blackfriars and Ludgate and Aldgate to be
dealt with in like manner? The firebrands of my soldiers
running under their thatches will only be half as hot, I think,
as the torches that Beelzebub is preparing for them below –
I suppose Beelzebub has been notified of the excommunication? It were better to leave nothing to chance in these
matters.

PANDULPH. I fancy Beelzebub has his own sources of informa-
tion, my Lord. In the meantime, your army –

JOHN. Is unpaid, disaffected, and not nearly large enough. We
will withdraw to the neighbourhood of Devizes and hope to
recover our strength.

    Exeunt.

SCENE FIVE

*View of London River, as before, but this time with the foreground
full of men-at-arms drawn oversize, drinking and quarrelling –
they wear the French Lilies on their coats.*

    Enter the DARK GIRL, *and the* RED-HAIRED GIRL, *with a
tambourine. The* DARK GIRL *sings, while her companion
dances and rattles her instrument, joining in the refrains.*

DARK GIRL (*singing – harshly and loudly*).

  Good people of London
  Come listen to me
  And I'll sing you a song
  Of our free liberty –
    Liberty liberty sign it and seal it
    Liberty liberty who dare repeal it?
  It was wrote out on paper
  What can we want more?
  Who cares for the Frenchmen,
  Who cares for the war?
    (*Refrain.*)
  Who cares for the Pope
  With his horns like old Moses,
  Or the King's hairy legs
  In a garden of roses?
    (*Refrain.*)
  Who cares for the larder
  All empty and bare,
  Who cares for the children
  With lice in their hair?
    (*Refrain.*)
  For they gave us sweet liberty
  To cuddle and love:
  What fairer companion
  Will dance to your grave –
    Liberty liberty sign it and seal it
          Who dare repeal it
          Touch it and feel it
          Meat drink, and fire
          True-lover's desire
    Liberty liberty all in the mire . . .

  Enter the MAYOR *and* YOUNG MARSHAL. *When they see*
  them, the GIRLS *run away.*

MAYOR. Look at them, my Lord, they know what they're up

to – they run away like rats as soon as they see me. It's not only that particular ditty, there's others as well, worse: there's a bad feeling in the streets. And I can't say that I blame them: they've heard enough pious pronouncements about liberty over the last twelve months to make the Fleet-ditch mudlarks vomit. You've uttered some of them yourself. So have I. But what have we got – in practical terms – to shew to the people? What bales of cloth, as it were, to lay upon my counter?

What d'ye lack, then what d'ye lack?
Sheets for your bed or shirts for your back?
Silk and satin, gay brocade
For wedding or for masquerade?

– it's just a little jargon, I made it up myself, my apprentices call it out at the shop-door, you know: it's supposed to attract the quality . . . Silk and satin indeed – it's laughable! I've had nothing in stock since the end of last summer but a hooligan army of drunken Northumbrians – yours.

YOUNG MARSHAL. Not mine, sir. De Vesci's: and most of them have gone.

MAYOR. It makes no great difference. We've been supplied with replacements. French, if you please. I'd call seven out of ten of them pickpockets and the other three pimps. Add to which, the danger.

YOUNG MARSHAL. Danger in defence of liberty –

MAYOR. The King will attack London, sir – as soon as he regroups his forces – and then where will we be with liberty signed and sealed? Where will my wife be, my thirteen-year-old daughter – I keep them locked up at home, which is good enough against the French. But the King has hungry wolves at his back who have had but the one meal, in the winter, and haven't eaten since . . . And the cook who must prepare for them has civic and commercial responsibility as well as his family – he has to weigh in his mind the virtues of freedom against the virtues of an ordered government. Which is what

we *may* get from this Prince Louis and his wife. But her
claim to the throne is not entirely satisfactory.

YOUNG MARSHAL. If John did in fact usurp his nephew
Arthur's crown, then –

MAYOR. But did he? It sticks in my memory he was chosen
king by your father and the barons for what seemed at the
time sufficient reason. If it was sufficient then, it should be
sufficient now. You can't change kings as though they were
mats upon the floor, you know: once you call a man a king,
you confirm it – with a sacrament. Which brings me to
another matter – what about the Pope?

YOUNG MARSHAL. That is unfortunate.

MAYOR. It is more than unfortunate. I've heard it said that by
an act of excommunication he has put us, as it were, upon
the dark side of the moon, and people think that's uncanny.
I think it's uncanny: I would prefer to be out of it.

   Enter FITZWALTER, *talking with* LOUIS *and* BLANCHE.

FITZWALTER. This is not what you were brought here for.

LOUIS. Those who pay the piper must call the tune, I suppose?
But what, my Lord, if the piper is considerably stronger than
his audience? King John has proved himself unable to
remove my army from your shores – are you likely to do any
better? I think not. My wife means to be Queen of England:
and if she *is* Queen, she will expect to reward those French
Lords that have helped her. You do not imagine they defied
excommunication for the mere pleasure of battle?

FITZWALTER (*coming across to* YOUNG MARSHAL). This
might have been foreseen – de Vesci no doubt would have
foreseen it, himself, if he hadn't decided to go north and
help the Scots. But I did not think they would have been
quite so direct. Nor so quick neither.

YOUNG MARSHAL. What are you talking about?

FITZWALTER. What do you think? He wants castles, he wants
manor-houses, for his serjeants, his pioneers, his camp-cooks,
his sutlers – God, he wants the land of England, boy! Do

you know what it was told me that he said to his wife there – that he looked upon us as no better than flamboys to light the doorway of his hall for one evening and then be quenched in the cesspool! Why isn't de Vesci here? He's dead – did you know that?

YOUNG MARSHAL. No.

FITZWALTER. Well, he is, you can have his wife now any time you care to ask her, if the King's not got in first . . . He was killed by an arrow at Barnard Castle. And he goes straight to hell as well, that's all in the Pope's bargain. (*To* LOUIS.) I would prefer to discuss this business, Your Grace, when the war is won and not before. By which time, I suppose, there will be no lands left in England capable of supporting a root of wild burdock. (*Exit.*)

BLANCHE (*to* YOUNG MARSHAL). I am sorry your colleague should have taken offence. But surely you must know that whether you choose to serve King Log or King Stork, the pond will be encumbered. Such is the price that little frogs must pay.

   Exeunt BLANCHE *and* LOUIS.

MAYOR. Did you tell me, my Lord, that the Lady Blanche has promised to ratify the Charter – if she becomes Queen?

YOUNG MARSHAL. She did make some, provisional, under-taking – after a fashion, yes.

MAYOR. A French fashion.

YOUNG MARSHAL. Yes . . . Log or Stork, did she say? At any rate the Log has my own father's legs astride of it. Perhaps I had better remember whose subject I was born. Clearly you cannot accompany me to Devizes, but when I have told him your sentiments, I think the King will keep his wildfire out of London.

MAYOR. Goodbye, my Lord – God go with you. It would be an uncouth irony indeed if the very man who built it should be the first one to cry –
'London Bridge is broken down

broken down
broken down . . .'

Exit MAYOR.

SCENE SIX

A picture of lords and ladies feasting in the open air. (This should somewhat resemble the grouping of actors in the beginning of Act II Scene 4.)

YOUNG MARSHAL (*picking up the* MAYOR's *last words*).

'London Bridge is broken down
                broken down
London Bridge is broken down
Dance over my Lady Lee' . . .

He walks backwards and forwards about the stage. He is still wearing Lady de Vesci's kerchief.

Enter LADY DE VESCI.

LADY DE VESCI. Your Lady Lee, if that is what you call her, is astonished that you have so long continued to wear her token, when you have fought all this while upon the adverse party. Do you bring it back to me to tell me you will wear it no longer because you have heard my husband is dead, and therefore your chivalric passion is necessarily blunted?

YOUNG MARSHAL. Madam, I confess that in these wars a knight of true courtesy is not able with confidence to devote his military conduct to the fame of any lady. The wars are dishonourable, being founded upon broken oaths, on both sides broken oaths. But I continue to wear your kerchief, with your permission, in order to shew that I am cognisant of a beautiful ideal over and above the petty treacheries of the time. In any case, I continue to love you in a very correct form – for I believe you to be unattainable. Are you not Caesar's?

She extends her hand and he kneels to kiss the tips of her fingers.

G

Enter JOHN *with* MARSHAL *and* OFFICERS.

JOHN. Caesar has indeed put his bridle upon her – his gold chain round her waist, etcetera . . . Are you come to Devizes to win her, or what?

YOUNG MARSHAL. No, my Lord: I am come to offer you my services.

JOHN. Offer? Young man, they are *required!* But never mind, never mind, we are very glad to have you – Marshal, a fatted calf, make it ready, have you got one – every day brings home the foolish prodigals . . . What was the matter then? You found the needles in Blanche's embroidery-box a bit too sharp for your fingers – hey? Well, go on, Marshal, embrace your errant offspring.

MARSHAL. My Lord, he has returned to his allegiance: but he should never have left it. I am pleased to see him here: I am not overjoyed. You may kiss me, my boy. I acknowledge you as mine once more.

A formal kiss between father and son.

JOHN. Affecting – very. Now: here is the situation. (*At map.*) The King of Scots has got to Lincoln, he must never reach London. So we strike eastwards, in between, occupy Cambridge, relieve the siege of Lincoln and, ah, liberate the men of Norfolk. I have my army in good heart at last: I even found some money for them: I have no doubt of victory.

YOUNG MARSHAL. Do you intend to burn London?

JOHN. Of course, of course, of course.

YOUNG MARSHAL. The Londoners, my lord, would declare for you at once, if you promised to spare their city.

JOHN. Oh they would? Are you sure? They are Englishmen after all, then? Well, we must see what we can do. A calculated clemency, Marshal – do you think that it would work?

LADY DE VESCI. Clemency can never be calculated. Like all other virtues, it must arise in full freedom out of the free heart of the man that proposes it – if it does not do that, it is no longer a virtue.

JOHN. Is that a satirical platitude, or is it supposed to be true?
By God, do you know – if it were true, we would have to
reconsider a great many deeds that have been done, in past
time, for the benefit of mankind, and acclaimed, what is
more, throughout the Old Testament and the New. What
about the Charter? I think you could call that a calculated
act of virtue – couldn't you? Couldn't you? . . .
The Liberation of Norfolk, completed in mid-October, 1216,
is an item of military history of no great consequence whatever. So off you go – get on with it.

Exeunt MARSHAL *and* YOUNG MARSHAL, *and* OFFICERS.
And although it must take its necessary place in any drama-
tization of the life and death of me, no doubt we can leave it
alone for the moment. It is, after all, in good hands . . .

SCENE SEVEN

No picture – bright lights, possibly house-lights up.
JOHN. There comes a time in any stage-play, when the stage
itself, the persons upon it, the persons in front of it, must
justify their existence – and I think this is the time now:
because on the 18th of October, I have to die, suffering from
a surfeit of cider and peaches, which is a great joke of
course, for I shall be taken short in the very moment of
neither victory nor defeat – my frantic history suspended
under circumstances of absolute inconclusion – King John
yet again too late to control his situation. A time, I say, must
come, when we stand in complete bewilderment as to what
we are doing here at all. I mean – what use is this –
He takes off his sword and throws it away, out of sight.
Or this –
Same business with his crown.
Or this –
Same business with his mantle.

– as a means of convincing you of the human importance of what we are talking about? What use am I myself – a bogey-man or ghost seven hundred and fifty years old and still mouldering – set down to prance before you in someone else's body? What in fact have you seen tonight?

A document signed, and nobody knew what for – or at least, nobody knew or could possibly know the ultimate conse-sequences thereof. A document repudiated, and nobody knew what for. A villainous king and his villainous barons sprinkling each other's blood all over the map. A good Archbishop disgraced. A sagacious Pope flung all cack-handed in the Vatican by contradictory letters continually coming in on every post, from an island which he might be pardoned for believing had never been properly converted in the first place. And finally, a few little tit-bits of scandal not even proved to be historically true.

He points to the Lady.

I mean her, for instance. She was a rumour in certain circles in the thirteenth century, to her husband she was a pretext for a grievance: and that's about her lot. Or so you might believe. Because this play concerns Magna Carta, and Magna Carta only. The lady is peripheral. A thoroughly masculine piece of work was Magna Carta – a collaborative effort between brutal military aristocrats and virgin clergy: as you will appreciate, when I read you a certain clause from it.

He finds a scroll of the Charter behind PANDULPH's *chair.*

Yes: you saw me tear it up at the end of the Second Act, but I kept another copy. I always twist around, you see, I plant one or two careful feet, carefully behind me, in my own footsteps, as I walk . . .

He opens the Charter:

'Paragraph 54:

No-one shall be arrested or imprisoned on the appeal of a woman for the death of any person except her own husband.'

Now this, granted its historical context, may make perfectly good sense. Dr William Sharp McKechnie, in his definitive work upon the subject of the Charter . . .

PANDULPH *enters, hands* JOHN *a book with a page marked, and sits down in his chair, where he busies himself with his papers.*

Ah, thank you. There's nothing peripheral about you, is there? You hieratic analytical rat-nosed porcupine – I am delivering the antidote to all those circles with no kinks in, that you treated us to at the beginning – remember?

He opens the book at the marked page:

Dr McKechnie, to return to the main issue, says that the object of Paragraph 54 was –

'to find a remedy for what the barons evidently considered an unfair advantage enjoyed by women appellants, who were allowed to appoint some champion to act for them in the 'duellum' – or trial by combat – while the accused man had to fight for himself.'

In other words –

Again pointing to the Lady:

– if she had a brother who was murdered by an enemy, and if she believed, sweet innocent, that she could get that enemy done-for by setting-on young Marshal to fight him in the lists with her scarf upon his headpiece – then by God she is in error! The Age of Chivalry is dead – 1215. And so, of course, in 1965, is Paragraph 54. If the whole of the Charter was compiled in that spirit, you would not be here tonight. (I am not going to even try to read you what it says about the Jews, let alone attempt to argue for it. Those of you who may be of that faith and nation would hardly have done worse under Adolf Hitler himself than under the pioneers of liberty who set their hand to this!) But you do see what I mean, – the lady is peripheral, both to the play and to the document.

Yet nevertheless she exists. And the very fact of such

existence is worth taking notice of. If she now stands in the middle of the stage it is not, I assure you, for reasons of fashionable immorality – it could just as well be my Queen here at this moment: but the Queen is in Gloucester, a place of security away from the war, looking after my young son; therefore we have the other woman, and it makes but little difference. For both ladies have been created in the image of God, they are females, of good health and comparative beauty . . . But we are not now discussing sexual attraction. Though of course it can never be entirely eliminated.

Nor should it be – it is part of her manifest corporal mechanism and has been given in a greater or less degree to every creature that walks. I wonder how she does walk? – two legs are common property, but to support a whole body, successfully, without conscious art and effort – did you ever see such a thing as a two-legged stool? And then she has her buttocks, above the legs, to sit on – but also to give pleasure to the eyes and to the touch. She has a womb which has brought forth more than one living child. She has her breasts which have afforded abundant nourishment to those children. She has her bowels and her heart and her lungs, her hands, her arms, her shoulders, her neck. And on her neck – look how it balances! – so small and delicate an egg of bone that I can almost encompass it within my ten fingers, and yet it is quite heavy and contains much that should give us pause. For by means of this egg alone can this creature eat, drink, talk, breathe, smell, see, weep, laugh, hear, and above all, think! Which is essential to her life – but what about the great rope of golden hair that hangs upon the egg? Here is nothing essential – here is decoration and delight – here is pure gratuity. Shave it off and yet she would function as before. Leave it on, comb it loose, braid it up, twist it round, let the wind blow through it, feel it, stroke it, look at it – who does not like to look at it? Yet the body of an eagle or an antelope or a toad could be similarly extolled. How are we to appreciate that she belongs to a unique species? She has a mind: and it has been educated with just that end in view.

LADY DE VESCI. First I was taught how Lucifer rebelled against his God and fell to hell: next how he tempted Eve: next how there is a difference between a mortal and a venial sin: after that there were some details of the life of Our Lord and His Mother, subordinated always to the prime importance of my own hypothetical chastity and how it must be preserved.

JOHN. By whom were you instructed!

LADY DE VESCI. Those who had Authority.

JOHN. Is that what they had? But then you defied your husband, you inspired a genuine if ridiculous devotion in the breast of at least one good-hearted young gentleman, and you became the most favoured subject of your ill-favoured luckless King. She followed in fact the very pattern of this Lucifer she had been warned against when young. Does her uniqueness lie in this then, that she is so easily lost? Much as we would value a diamond or an amethyst which a crack in the floorboards or a thick heap of leaves on the ground could take away from us for ever? If such is her condition she must not remain anonymous. Her name is Margaret, and her father— which will surprise you – was King William the Lion of Scotland. She is illegitimate, of course – but it does fit the picture. Why else has the atrocious Eustace met his death at Barnard Castle in the north, except that he was helping his half-brother-in-law, the present King Alexander, to reduce my own poor royalty? And why else would she be so disinclined to obey his commands?

LADY DE VESCI. I will tell you why else. Because he demanded my obedience. He maintained he had Authority.

JOHN. So he had – you were his wife. Is not that so, Master Legate?

PANDULPH. Yes.

JOHN. A marriage is an oath taken before God – it enjoins obedience upon the inferior party and constant faith upon both parties. So do the oaths taken between kings and their noblemen, and between noblemen and their dependants. Am I right, Pandulph?

PANDULPH. Yes.

JOHN. There is a failure in logic here. Can you put your finger on it?

LADY DE VESCI. Yes, I can. You have condoned my disobedience to Lord Eustace –

JOHN. He laid violent hands upon you –

LADY DE VESCI. That should not have been relevant. You also condoned one or two adulteries on the part of your Queen.

JOHN. I was in love with her.

LADY DE VESCI. But you refused to condone the rebellion of your barons. So far as the doctrine of Authority – either in marriage or statecraft – was convenient to yourself, you insisted upon it: and where it was not, you ignored it.

JOHN. Exactly so! Inconsistent, irregular, unreasonable. And this is our uniqueness. Not in our capacity for damnation or salvation nor yet in our capacity for logical rationality – though both of them are glorious: and both of them, I fear, have distorted our nature. Indeed I am inclined to think, that not only are you unsuited to be a married woman and I to be a king, but that none of us, ever, are suited to be either.

PANDULPH. But you *were* a king, my Lord.

JOHN. God's Teeth, yes, I was, I was – and what did I do with it? I spoiled the Egyptians, Pandulph, that's what I did – I made use of my sacred station for promiscuous enjoyment – not always for myself: look at London Bridge, very useful – and beautiful . . . but, by and large, in this world of constructed Authority which is Egypt of the taskmasters, I played the part of sly escapist Israel – and I nearly got away. Do you want to know the name of Pharaoh? Old hard-heart on his chariot, stuck fast in the quicksand? They call him

Pope Innocent, and you are his servant, and you are also my dupe! Because I do not believe, not one iota, no, in the Authority which you claim, which is claimed in this Charter, and which is claimed by the golden crown I have this very moment doffed!

    I do not feel very well.
My bowels are rolling over
Like the first pull on a great bell.
Not only in my kingdom
Are there civil disturbances
The members of my own body
Are bringing forth their grievances . . .

Never mind, it has passed . . . So what have you got to say to me, Egyptian?

PANDULPH. At this late stage, nothing that could be of any use to you. But it is a truth and I know it to be a truth, that the unity of all men is desired by Christ, within Christ: that we are subordinate to Christ and yet will become part of Him: and both the subordination and incorporation are mirrored upon earth. Church, State, and Family are all ordained microcosms of the hierarchy of heaven – just imagine us without them? Where would we be? Choked and lacerated by the brambles of our own appetites – our animal appetites which we share with the eagle, the antelope, and the toad. We would be both barren and over-luxuriant at one and the same time. And yet this can be prevented – a good gardener can prevent it, he can weed, prune and culti-vate, impose in fact Authority. *You* are a dandelion.

JOHN. I am partial to dandelions. Coarse in texture I know, and the scent is undistinguished and they are far too prolific. But powdered across the slope of a green meadow, all those thousand dots of gold – who could want to be rid of them? Even to give place to violets? In any case, despite all your efforts, Pandulph, Authority does not remain as it was – it changes a little, and where it changes it can also be mitigated.

He holds up the Charter.

Authority of the Crown gives way bit by bit to Authority of the Common Law. But even the Law, liberally administered, can one day say to this woman – 'Shave off your hair'. And it will give good reasons: and she will have to do it. What it will never say and can never say, is – 'Here is a cloth-of-gold ribbon, which enhances your hair. Put it on, and I will adore you.' Now, which is better – to have this head shaved by order of the Law, or by the violence of my hand?

PANDULPH. If the Law ordered it, presumably it would have been for the general benefit. If you were to do it by yourself, only you would be satisfied. Obviously the first is better. You are wasting my time.

He turns to his papers and takes little more notice.

JOHN.

Once again my bowels roll over.
What is there inside me I have yet to discover?
Too many women, I think,
Too much food and drink . . .

She will still be bald, whether it is the first or the second! And I have an amorous nature, therefore it is far more likely I would offer her the ribbon. Of course, I have been cruel: but only because the ordained microcosms that you talked about have somehow suffered disruption. Or have they perhaps created disruption by their very existence? Anyhow, it has been because of them that I have had to do the things that made me hated. Had they never been imposed upon the world – but we advance no further, do we? You are not even listening. You are quite right, of course – why should you damned well listen – while the world is as it is, you have the best argument! The lion and the lamb cannot lie down together –

PANDULPH (*a brief glance up and back to his papers*). Until the Second Coming.

JOHN. Which may very well happen before these people here even reach their places of work tomorrow morning! And when it does happen, who will know it? The First Coming was recognized by twelve poor yokels only – and it tormented one of them to the extent of thirty silver pennies and a long rope to hang himself.

> A rope around the neck and
> A rope around the bell:
> Why do they have to give such a
> Terrible strong pull?

Who will be Judas next time? Unpredictable me or Pandulph the microcosmic gardener? But, as we stand now, the lion must be kept in chains and the lamb in a secure sheepfold. I have given thought to both necessities. Consider this clause –

Reading from the Charter:

And no free man shall be arrested or imprisoned . . . except . . .

you have heard it spoken twice already. And also the other one –

To no man will we sell or deny right and justice . . .

No detail, no precision, no temporary or feudal pettifogging that can fix these two clauses in the early thirteenth century or in any other century, yet they can find a home in all. My work, d'you see – not the Archbishop's nor the Marshal's, and certainly not Fitzwalter's. I said: make those clauses general – lax, if you like – because by their very laxity they go some way to admit the existence of dandelions, of disobedient women, and ribbons of cloth-of-gold.

Interpret them how you like –

LADY DE VESCI. I tried to interpret one of them –

JOHN. Yes, and you were denied your interpretation: but you were quite right and your husband was wrong. Interpret them how you like, and agreed that they concede the Authority of the Law, not one act of injustice, interpret them how you like, can ever be done, ever that will not be contrary to so general a clause. I gave them to you all, and all of you can use them – against the Barons, or the Bishops, or even the Crown, against the Parliaments, the Scriveners, the Catchpolls, the Beadles and the Bailiffs, the Marshals and their Serjeants – indeed, every single stone, brick, or granule of aggregate that help to build the buttresses which hold up the walls of the Temple of Authority are in peril from these clauses! Every buttress must be made afraid of you – and you must never fear the buttress: because a buttress is a dead thing, inert, fabricated, the result of a delusion – whereas you are men and women – I have shewn you your pattern, here –

He points to the Lady.

– and the pattern for her was God. But I am not capable of talking about God. Pandulph has reconstituted God as if God was a sack of Portland Cement – mix it up with water, it will stand hard for generations, you can chip the bits off, but you cannot remodel it. Never let that be said of this parchment – I warn you! And as you have all come here in some sort of celebratory and congratulatory frame of mind, I will also give a warning to the parchment itself:

'Woe unto you when all men speak well of you.'

He rolls the Charter up.

Pandulph, my throat is dry,
Grey patches are trickling over
The clear pupil of my eye.
I am not very well and I feel a kind of dizziness:
Pandulph have you no answer to my tortuous eloquence?
You consequential nosey-parker
I am waiting for your answer!

PANDULPH. Thou fool, this night thy soul shall be required of thee.

He gathers up his papers and goes.

SCENE EIGHT

A large-scale map of the Wash.
JOHN. The first thing they ever taught you –
LADY DE VESCI. Was how Lucifer invented sin.
JOHN.

> As for example, gluttony . . .
> I have been the guest, in Norfolk,
> Of the loyal citizens of Lynn.
> They were not very wise in their good hospitality.
> Great vats of stewed peaches and new cider to drink:
> The cider was very gassy
> And the peaches were too pink.

I don't think you should be here – we have a long march this morning – keep your bed, be comfortable . . .

He finds his mantle and sword and assumes them again – not the crown. He strides about the stage, shouting:

Come on come on, come on, October the 12th, 1216, past four o'clock on a filthy wet morning, get your feet on the floor – bugler, where's the call?

Bugle calls and drums start to beat.

> Keep your bed, lady, keep it
> Be cosy while you can –
> Warm blankets for the warm woman
> And a hard horseback for her man.

He leads the lady off, tenderly kissing her hand: and then returns to his bustling. He holds the rolled-up Charter in his left hand rather like a truncheon.

Colour party, forward! Marshal, where are you? We're on the move already!

The stage begins to fill with the confusion of an army breaking camp – as many persons as can be found, as OFFICERS, SOLDIERS, WAGGONERS and so forth . . . flags, drums, kitbags, weapons of all sorts. Practicable wagons are dragged

*on to the stage — they seem very heavy and are being man-
handled with difficulty.*

MARSHAL *and* YOUNG MARSHAL *enter.*

MARSHAL. I want all the transport over the mudflats before
the tide comes in!

YOUNG MARSHAL. Waggoner-serjeant, why aren't those
wheels turning? Get on with it, man!

FIRST OFFICER. What time is low water?

SECOND OFFICER. Twelve o'clock by the book — we've got
plenty of time.

JOHN. Oh no we have not, we have never got that!

OFFICERS (*generally*). Come on, come on . . . heave, you stupid
Dutchmen, heave . . . *etc.*

JOHN. What's holding it up? Why won't that wagon move?

*What began as confused but comparatively purposeful move-
ment has now bogged down completely.*

A SOLDIER. This mud's more soft than we thought — we can't
get a purchase.

JOHN. Late again, late, you are always too late — we are march-
ing upon my London —

I will tolerate no delays!

My bowels are rolling over

In seventeen different ways

Oh peaches and new cider

And this disgusting muddy river . . .

There is a flow of water six inches deep pouring over my
ankles — *what* time did you say was the tide?

MARSHAL. It should still be running out.

JOHN. Running out? You incompetent antiquity — it's coming
in, fast! Ankles, calves, knees — do you want us to be
drowned! Clear that wagon — quick!

*In the middle of the stage they are all staggering as though
surrounded by swirling water. If possible an effect of shifting
eddies should be projected on the map of the Wash behind.*

SECOND OFFICER. Jesu Mercy, can the almanack be wrong?

JOHN. Of course it can be wrong. It was written by a bishop!

YOUNG MARSHAL. My Lord, it's no good – these are regular sea waves coming in now, and it's getting deeper every minute.

MARSHAL. We must abandon the wagons, my Lord, get the horses through first.

JOHN. Abandon my wagons – all my jewels are in that wagon – an emerald, a sapphire, a garnet and a topaz, that were sent to me by the Pope, a sapphire and a ruby I would have given to St Edmund but they were too beautiful to leave my hands – my crown and my sceptre – God's Bread, they were my perquisites, the mark of my authority, good God, I was the overseer . . .

He sinks on one knee, and supports himself on his hand.

MARSHAL. Hold up the King. He is falling in the deep mud.

OFFICERS *go to his help.*

SECOND OFFICER. My Lord, it is not the mud, it is mortal sickness that makes him fall.

FIRST OFFICER. He has lost consciousness, my Lord.

He has not in fact lost consciousness, but is now on all fours in the middle of the flood, fighting against it. The men who are helping him have a hard struggle, both against the water and against the weight of his body. MARSHAL *and* YOUNG MARSHAL *stand downstage, as it were upon dry land.* YOUNG MARSHAL *appears to be about to go and assist, but his father checks him quietly.*

MARSHAL. The waters have come over him as the Red Sea came over Pharaoh . . . My son, our new King Henry is not yet ten years old. He has succeeded to a kingdom all but swept away by deluge. I am too near my own grave to be able myself to dredge it up again for him. But one thing must be seen to. At his coronation, whatever the Church may say, he must take oath to observe the Great Charter. There is no other way by which the war can be stopped, the French driven out, and the King's people held together. Let it but

be done, my son, and the commonwealth may continue . . .
Help Landless John back
Onto his own dry land.
Never mind the wagons . . .
Unclench his cold left hand.

The OFFICERS *have brought* JOHN *ashore. One of them takes the scroll, with difficulty, from his hand and gives it to the* MARSHAL. *They carry his body off the stage, and all exeunt, leaving the wagons and gear amid the swirling water.*

Appendix

After I had completed the play, I remembered the legend of the Wise Men of Gotham, and regretted that I failed to insert it in my story. This scene, accordingly, is offered as an alternative to the greater part of Act Two Scene 4. Additional characters are:

A PARSON (of Gotham)

A FARMER

A SMITH

A MILLER.

(The other PARSON, the GOLDSMITH and his Wife, are consequently not used, if this episode is preferred.) Gotham is normally thought to be the Nottinghamshire township of that name. There was however another Gotham in Sussex, and I have the authority of the Oxford Book of Nursery Rhymes for adopting it.

Act Two

SCENE FOUR

A picture of a small hamlet, with church, cottages, and peasants carrying out their harvesting etc.

Enter PARSON, FARMER, SMITH *and* MILLER.

PANDULPH. Therefore, we must take care that the hostility maintained toward the King by both barons and superior clergy is not allowed to outweigh the genuine sentiments of loyalty which no doubt still burn within the breasts of the common people of England. Here, for example, we see the leading inhabitants of some small village, assembled together

H

with joy to welcome their Sovereign upon his progress. You, sir, are presumably the Parish Priest – the Parish priest of – where?

PARSON. Gotham, in the county of Sussex, my Lord. Here is Robin the Miller, Peter the Blacksmith, and John of the Manor Farm.

PANDULPH. Very good, very good, continue your preparations . . .

He busies himself with papers at his desk.

PARSON. Certainly he spent the last two days in Lewes. Where will he come next?

SMITH. My sister Edith whose good man, as you know, Parson, has a contract for leading the horse dung out of Lewes Castle stables, she sent word to me by my little nephew late in the evening that the word is all round Lewes he's for Pevensey today.

MILLER. He don't have to come through Gotham –

SMITH. He comes where he wants to come. He carries a hawk on his fist and many of his noblemen do likewise, and he follows the wild fowl where he rides, taking his needful journey and the exercise of his sport together. He has the Queen with him too and great ladies beside. You see the fine weather – he has time and leisure to diverge his course into whatsoever downs or meadows take his fancy.

FARMER. Aye or standing crops. We've not got our wheat in yet. I can't endure to have horsemen riding over that. There's ever furious ruffians will trample after the King where he goes – they take no account for nothing and then what will we do?

PARSON. There's another point to be made out of that, goodman Farmer. It's a matter of Law. Now I don't know and I've never heard it proved, according to document and precedent, and I don't hear that it was ever wrote down in pen and ink: but custom, I am told it is, a Norman custom brought by old King William, that wheresoever the King should ride, be it harvest corn or champaine pasture, that very road for ever after becomes a public road – the King's High Road, no less. Now some call that prerogative of royalty. I call it just plain abuse. But how do we prevent it?

MILLER. It should have been prevented in that Charter they made him set his seal to.

PARSON. Not in so many words it wasn't, Miller – I read it, when displayed in Chichester south aisle – it wasn't there.

SMITH. We can't take no chances. We can't let him through.

FARMER. We can't fight him, neither. He's the King, he takes his pleasure and his sport where he wants to, as was said.

PARSON. Suppose, though, upon his journey into Gotham he was to meet with but little pleasure – suppose it seemed a queer-like place for him to come to, and no great comfort for the ladies neither –

SMITH. No great comfort in my poor forge-house, certain: but they won't be wanting to take their dinners inside of there. I don't see how –

PARSON. I didn't mean comfort in the way of cushions and stools, Blacksmith, I meant comfort for the mind. Now a King in a rebellious land with a memory of excommunication – he needs ease for his spirit and for the discourse of his tender ladies. Now, suppose he thought the Devil ruled in Gotham?

FARMER. You mean witchcraft magic, Parson?

PARSON. Jesus Mary no – we'd imperil our immortal souls with that. Something of the nature, though – but gentler, d'you see, and safer, under God. Come here . . .

They get into a huddle and whisper with occasional bursts of laughter.

Enter the CLERK.

CLERK. Is this the village of Gotham? Excuse me, is this the village of Gotham, reverend sir?

PARSON. It is indeed, sir, Christ be with you, sir. Can I be of assistance to you, sir? Can I put you on your road?

CLERK. No no, I am already on it, thank you very much. I am a member of the Royal Household and I am commissioned to inform you that the King's Grace and the Queen's Grace with a considerable retinue intend very shortly to pass the bounds of this parish on their way to Pevensey Castle. No doubt, as the sun is already high in the heavens, the company will desire to eat their noontide meal. You must therefore expect some small levy to be made upon your hen-runs and pig-sties. Sucking-pigs? You have sucking-pigs? Good. The King's falconry has been successful this morning and there will be no shortage of game-birds. But I fancy the services of your good wives will be called upon for plucking and drawing and so forth. Also bread, if you have it, newly-baked. You will of course be paid for your trouble – more or less.

> *While he is talking to the Parson, the other three have gone off-stage and now return carrying a large wooden bowl or wash-tub, which they manhandle awkwardly, bumping into the* CLERK.

CLERK (*cont.*) Might I ask what you think you are doing with that bowl?

SMITH. It's a question, sir, of whether or no the King's Grace is partial to fish?

CLERK. It isn't Friday, is it?

SMITH. Ah sir, we're in Gotham here, all our days is like to be Friday here, sir. On account of the multitude of heavy fish that do befavour the seacoast downalong. We could catch his Grace a powerful draught thereof, if so be he had a taste for it.

CLERK. And how, sir, do you imagine you are going to catch fish in a bowl? I should have thought a net or line would be more appropriate.

MILLER. You think we're daft in Gotham, sir? We have nets and lines galore beside the shingle, sir, but this here bowl, sir, is the vessel we must sail in, for to seek God's fish upon

His waters. When the wind is fresh and lively and we three jolly lads aboard of her, she do heave and she do spin upon the tide most beautiful to be sure.

CLERK. Oh.

FARMER. Would you say the King, sir, was partial to fried fish?

CLERK. But – a boat, surely – you must have a boat?

PARSON. Boats gets wrecked, boats is feeble, frail. This here bowl, with the sacred words we do say over her, she should never wreck nor founder, never, in the service of the King.

CLERK. I fancy the King will confine himself to partridges.

PARSON. Then that being so, sir, there is no need for us to venture. Put it down, good men, and let us take our rakes and set once more to work.

They all collect rakes and go to a corner of the stage.

CLERK. Harvesting, already?

PARSON. No sir, but to rescue the life of a poor female creature in distress. See this dew-pond here, sir. Last night there was a sad discovery.

MILLER. The full moon, sir, out of heaven, we did observe she had fell in, and now by daylight we do rake for her to fetch her out and to restore her to her rightful place. You rake to the north, Peter Smith, and I to the south, and you, John Farmer, to the east, while Parson seeks for her upon the west-hand side. Rake, boys, rake.

They rake, singing 'Rake, boys, rake' in the manner of a chanty.

CLERK. I suppose you would think I was not quite in my right mind if I were to suggest that what you had seen had been no more than the usual reflection?

PARSON. That we would, sir, certain. For all know well enough the moon is insecurely fixed aloft or else why do she turn and turn so changeable every blessed month except as how the wind should waver her and so in wavering, bring her down maybe? Last night it was a stormy night indeed . . .

And when we've done this pond, Rob Miller, you and
Edward Carpenter must set about that fencing job around
the cuckoo's tree. Rake, boys, rake away . . .

CLERK. You might as well explain to me what is the cuckoo's
tree? I am after all a stranger in these parts.

SMITH. So fine a summer as it's been, sir, we can't endure to
see the winter come. Now winter comes when cuckoos are
flown away, and so we catch our cuckoo here, and set him in
a tree and fence him round with good split boards and there
he bides according. We're none too soon to do it neither, for
cuckoo's tune has changed already. Ah, we're sharp in
Gotham, sir: we can watch the devilments of Nature and
control them when they come.

CLERK. So it appears. I am not at all sure that the King's
Grace will be able to favour your village with his presence
after all. It may be necessary for him to push on to Pevensey
direct. But he will be informed of the loyal warmth and
traditional rustic good sense that obtains among the inhabitants here. Yes indeed. Good morning.

Exit CLERK.

PARSON. Boys, we've done it.

ALL. Arrh . . .

*They launch into a dance – a kind of morris dance using their
rakes (and if convenient) the bowl: singing . . .*

'Rake boys rake, the King is coming to Gotham

Rake boys rake, the King is going away.

Rake boys rake, the bowl is on the ocean

Rake boys rake, the cuckoo's in the tree . . .'

Exeunt dancing.

SCENE FIVE

Picture of apple orchard as in Act Two Scene 4 of original text;
Enter JOHN, QUEEN, LADY DE VESCI, MARSHAL, PRINCE
HENRY, CLERKS *and attendants.*

CLERK. I would not recommend Gotham, my Lord. Either they are up to some sort of dubious magic or else they are all astray in their wits. I fancy the latter. There is a great deal of intermarriage in these rural communities and it sometimes has curious effects.

JOHN. What effects?

CLERK. Three of them intended to put to sea in a bowl.

JOHN. Good God. Of course they might be brewing rebellion . . . Possible, do you think?

CLERK. No, my Lord. They are only silly country folk: but if they are indeed imbecile, there might be some unfortunate incident. The modesty of the ladies might perhaps be affronted, if you know what I mean . . .?

JOHN. I doubt if these ladies would mind that very much . . . But, eccentricity, though entertaining, is occasionally dangerous. I don't want to stamp it out – indeed I would welcome it – but on the south coast, in this month, in the present state of the kingdom – no, no, there are far too many untoward events taking place as it is. We will not go through Gotham.

QUEEN. But, my Lord, it might prove to be an agreeable and humorous experience.

JOHN. No! No, madam, no! There are plots against my life and against the life of my children. I have a mind to *burn* Gotham.

LADY DE VESCI. My Lord, we have no evidence they are in any conspiracy.

JOHN. Marshal, what do you think? Fire and sword, intimidation?

MARSHAL. Certainly not, my Lord. It would be the clearest contravention of the Charter of Liberties.

JOHN. Why yes, so it would . . . You put me to shame, Marshal. Let us forget about Gotham . . . We have travelled far enough this morning – let them serve us with a little food and drink.

From here on the scene follows the original Act Two Scene 4 until line 26 on page 60.

(By so much the less
Was I truly a king)

The ensuing Goldsmith episode is then omitted: and the play continues as before from the entry of YOUNG MARSHAL on page 64. The only alterations necessary in the retained dialogue of the original scene are:

Page 58 line 11: Omit 'Kentish'.

Page 65 line 25: For 'Kentish Coast' read 'Southern Coast'.

Methuen's Modern Plays

EDITED BY JOHN CULLEN

Henry Livings	*Kelly's Eye and other plays*
	Eh?
John Mortimer	*Lunch Hour and other plays*
	Two Stars for Comfort
Harold Pinter	*A Slight Ache and other plays*
	The Birthday Party and other plays
	The Caretaker
	The Collection and The Lover
	The Homecoming
Jean-Paul Sartre	*Crime Passionel*
Theatre Workshop and Charles Chilton	*Oh What a Lovely War*

★   ★   ★

Other Plays from Methuen

Jean Anouilh	*Dinner With the Family*
	Restless Heart
	Thieves' Carnival
John Arden	*Ironhand*
	(an adaptation of Goethe's *Goetz von Berlichingen*)
Bertolt Brecht	*Plays Volume I*
	(The Caucasian Chalk Circle, The Threepenny Opera, The Trial of Lucullus, The Life of Galileo)
	Plays Volume II
	(Mother Courage, St Joan of the Stockyards, The Good Person of Szechwan)
Henry Chapman	*You Won't Always Be On Top*
*Euripides	*The Trojan Women*

*In preparation

Max Frisch	*Three Plays*
	(The Fire Raisers, Count Oederland, Andorra)
Jean Giraudoux	*Duel of Angels*
	Plays Volume I
	(Tiger at the Gates, Duel of Angels, Judith)
Gordon Honeycombe	*The Redemption*
	(Adapted from five mediaeval cycles of plays)
John Millington Synge	*The Playboy of the Western World*
	Plays and Poems
Oscar Wilde	*Lady Windermere's Fan*
	The Importance of Being Earnest

★   ★   ★

Books on Theatre from Methuen

Leo Aylen	*Greek Tragedy and the Modern World*
★Eric Bentley	*The Life of the Drama*
Bertolt Brecht	*Brecht on the Theatre*
Robert Brustein	*The Theatre of Revolt*
Jan Kott	*Shakespeare Our Contemporary*
Irene Mawer	*The Art of Mime*
Charles Marowitz, Tom Milne, Owen Hale	*The Encore Reader*
C. B. Purdom	*A Guide to the Plays of Bernard Shaw*
Marc Slonim	*Russian Theater*
John Russell Taylor	*Anger and After*
John Willett	*The Theatre of Bertolt Brecht*

★In preparation